THE RAINBOW BRIDGE
The Shakta Tantrika of the Uttarakaulas

JOHN POWER
and introduction by GREGORY PETERS

Phoenix of Chelmsford
2020
ISBN: 978-0-9542286-3-7

Uttarakuru and the Rainbow Bridge

In Uttarakuru, prepare to meet the Goddess....and the Gods
They are in your deep mind
That gives form to the forces of nature
No two people see the same.
Tantrika is transformation
Prepare to dive deep
And find your own divinity within.

Contents:

Preface:

The Rainbow Bridge is a piece of symbolism from Norse mythology used by Guru Dadaji Mahendranath [1911- 1991] to signify the joining of Eastern and Western paganism, which we have chosen as equally symbolic as a title for this collection of writings.

As much of the history of Dadaji has been written before, and his essays are easily found circulating on the Internet I would like to point to some more recent research here so as not to be too repetitive. Two people who have scoured internet sources of information about Dadaji's story are Andrew Stenson of Amookos: the Arcane Magical Order of the Knights of Shambala, and a woman who prefers to be anonymous, once a member of Amookos, and whose internet study is quite extensive due to her interest in genealogy. Amookos was a group established in 1978 by Dadaji and Mike Magee as a Westernised form of the Adi Nath Indian tradition, largely Shaivite in nature: of the God Siva in the Indian mainstream, after Goraksnath, but as 'Adi', or original, Nath is said to stem from Goraknath's Kaula guru, Matsyendranath, and that was the end of the tradition that Dadaji had been initiated into. In tandem he also created a Westernised form of the Uttarakaula, North Indian, Goddess-centred, tradition that he considered his other most important initiation and which he asked me to help him spread. The researchers discovered the details of Lawrence, aka Anton, Miles, as Dadaji was from his birth in the East End of London in 1911; his work as a painter and decorator; marriage; birth of a son, who survives him; his life as Socialist/Communist activist; army career as a physiotherapist that included service in the Spanish Civil War; and his emigration to Australia, in the deal referred to as '£10 Poms' as that was the cost of the voyage, but should have had a minimum 10 year stay as part of the deal, which Lawrence ignored, as it acted instead as a stepping stone to his travels in the orient.

Alongside his worldly career of course Lawrence was motivated by his inner spiritual life, having been born into a maternal family line that gave him a Great Aunt, 'Clay' Palmer, who lived in Rottingdean, near Brighton in Sussex on England's South coast. Pagans tend to steer clear of Christian clerics and churches, and there is no record of Clay in Rottingdean church archives or graveyard, but the Palmer name is associated with the South coast area and includes Samuel Palmer [1805-81], the mystical painter from Shoreham, in Kent, neighbouring county to Sussex that may prove to be a better place to hunt for record of her, although Clay is a pseudonym meaning Sword. Clay did however initiate young Lawrence into witchcraft at the age of 11 in Rottingdean, which is also where there is one of the homes of Rudyard Kipling, whose books set in India in the days of the Raj would have provided inspiration to young Lawrence for exotic travels. There is ample evidence of Dadaji's involvement in witchcraft elsewhere, in his involvement with Gerald Gardner, the founder of Modern Witchcraft, at his Brickett Wood coven and nudist centre in Hertfordshire. Gardner claimed that his contact with hereditary witches had begun in the New Forest in Hampshire, the next county west of Sussex on the South Coast.

Another 'infamous' occultist that Dadaji met near the end of his life in Brighton, as well as London, was Aleister Crowley, who died in nearby Hastings on the South Coast. By his own account in 'Sothis' magazine in 1978 he spoke to Crowley after the trial brought against him by Nina Hammett, which bankrupted him and contributed to the move out of London for financial reasons. By that stage of his life Crowley was a heroin junkie, and they are not known for reliability. His social group had been upper crust socialites, and several of us have searched his diaries of that period, but no painter and decorators are recorded. The only Lawrence referred to is said to be Laurence Felkin. When I met

Van Morrison at an exhibition I remember the conversation clearly, I doubt it would have remained with Van long. Similarly conversations with a decorator interested in witchcraft and Crowley's 'Book of the Law' would probably not warrant recording by an ageing junkie. But Dion Fortune also met Crowley at this time and said he still bore the signs of a magus. Dadaji regarded him as a Taoist scholar, who was then working on the Thelemite translation of the 'I Ching' oracle. He also apparently advised Dadaji to travel to the Orient to extend his studies of this, which he did, and became an I Ching Master and Taoist Priest in Malaysia. Crowley also told him of prominent characters from Nepal, from his mountain climbing days, to contact as well.

After Crowley's death Dadaji camped out in Epping Forest, just East of London, where part of his paternal family line lived, for a personal vision quest, before he formed his plan to travel east via the cheap Australian route. In Australia he was recorded in the local press at various times as being in the Buddhist Society and also as a witch, who had known Crowley. He met Rosaleen Norton, but described her as 'an astral junkie'. His crossover to Asia saw him studying Thai witchcraft, near the River Kwai and elsewhere; becoming a Taoist Priest and 'I Ching' master in Malaysia; was initiated into Nikaya Theravada Buddhism in Sri Lanka as Mahinda, the same name in Pali as his later Mahendra in the Nath sect; and at the other end of the Indian sub-continent, in Bhutan, became a Maha Lama of the Karguyt-Pas sect as Thalwai Wangpo Rimpoche.

The first of the two initiations he held in the highest regard, however, came when he first set foot on the dock at Bombay [Mumbhai] on the full Moon day of July in 1953, which in local custom is known as Guru Purnima: the day when Hindus venerate their teachers, and he was to meet Sri Lokanath, Digambar-Avadhut of Uttarakashi [in North India] who he held in great esteem until 1960 and Lokanath's death, and indeed after. This was the man who initiated Dadaji into the Adi Nath sect. In a country where oral tradition has been the norm between gurus and their pupils and at a time before modern communication technology, it is not surprising to find certain identification of this man. Dadaji said that he was the last of the line of the Adi Nath tradition that originated with Matsyendranath, a Kaula Tantrik, as seen in the book ascribed to him: 'The Kaula-Jnana Nirnaya', which was said to be written in the 12th century C.E, although there are references to him in the earlier writings of Abvinavagupta of Kashmir, and Matseyhendranath's best known pupil Goraksnath has been dated to the 11th century. Goraksnath transformed the Nath tradition into a monastic Order in Nepal and North India. Much is recorded at Pashupatinath Temple near Kathmandu, but no mention is made of Matseyendranth as a founder of the Adi Naths, causing Mike Magee to pronounce it a 'bogus tradition'. In truth it was probably rather set up by followers. The sect was known to have inhabited one of the temples at the complex of highly erotically sculpted site at Khajivaho, in Madya Pradesh, which is long since deserted. Thereby is a clue as to why the evidence for the sect is scarce. Mogul and British Raj Christians have for many centuries done much to suppress the joyous cosmology of native tribes and succeeded to the point where couples are not now allowed to kiss in Bollywood films! The occupying powers would have taken more kindly to Goraksnath's transformation, and 21st century Naths are celibate, so do not breed female Naths!

The second initiation that Dadaji was so proud to have bestowed on him took place in the Kali Temple in the town of Ranchi, about 200 miles west of Kolkata in Bihar State, and was given by Pagalababa [the 'mad father'] of the Uttarakaula Tantriks. Dadaji gave no date for this auspicious occasion, but said that after his Nath initiation in 1953 he travelled outside India to some of the places mentioned above, then wandered around Bengal and Bihar before that meeting and initiation took place. We can thank also Canadian initiate Kristen Godfrey, for her Indian travels and resulting research that found a surviving Native Indian of the Uttarakaula tradition, who Dadaji was unaware of, in the shape of Kulavadhut of Sikkim, who had been initiated by Maheshwari Ma, and who, like Pagalababa, had been initiated by the same preceding guru, Thakar Kalachand. Kristen met Kulavadhut in Gangtok, Sikkim, but accounts of both Pagalababa and Maheshwari Ma can be found in Indian publications. So where Dadaji had on occasions mentioned a merger between Naths and Uttarakaulas, he was not in a position to make such a decision. The Westernised adaptations of these two traditions he created remain just that, and a native Uttarakaula tradition continues, with Kulavadhut aware of his Westernised associates. If we also take Yogiraj Gurunath Siddhinath, who Dadaji initiated, into account so does a native Adi Nath lineage continue, but in his book *'Wings of Freedom'* [Alight Publications, 2005] he recalls a later native guru, Babaji, rather than Dadaji. Much of the information that Dadaji gave me in 1979 for the Uttarakaula transformation he wished to see for the West was never published in the 1970s or 80s and so never found its way into collections of his writings, but it has formed the structure of the Fellowship of Uttara Circles of Kaulas that emerged.

It can be seen from the dates given above that Dadaji reached the age of 80, but suffered strokes which impaired his mental functions near the end of that life. Amookos developed well in England from 1978 to 1989, with tentacles reaching out into the U.S., Europe and salient other countries until disaster struck and Dadaji, with his impaired memory and associated confusion, decided that progress with Amookos was not in line with his aims. An example of his memory loss was that he had asked Mike Magee, who had been appointed Head of the Order, to write grade papers, like those in pseudo-masonic orders, for students wishing to join the order. Mike had done this and sent them to Dadaji for his approval, which he had given, and the first three grade were published in 1982 as *'Tantra Magick'*. However by 1989 Dadaji had no memory of having seen them. Letters were also sent accusing Mike of having undertaken a Christian wedding, which was untrue, and was a confusion about another Amookos member. These and other crazinesses Mogg Morgan has recorded in a chapter called 'When Your Guru Goes Gaga' in a book of his titled *'Tantra Sadhana'*. To add insult to injury, Dadaji had been involved in a correspondence with American John Pilskog, editor of a magazine called, ironically, 'Open Door' and appointed him to lead a group called the International Order of Naths, which eventually became the INO, or International Nath Order, and all Amookons were expected to take a new form of initiation, along with other new members and regard John Pilskog as Supremo. Naturally that went down like a lead balloon, and created a great Anglo-American schism of the two groups. Within two years Dadaji had had his final stroke and died, but in those two years he had been persuaded by Mr. Pilskog to sign a copyright agreement about his collections of writings when previously he had wanted these essays given the widest possible dispersion. Obviously a measure more of a control mechanism than about Enlightenment: creating a closed door rather than an 'open door', as the documents became altered in favour of INO, and only available with their approval.....or that would have been the case if not for the internet.

Meanwhile I had told Dadaji that I was tired of the hassles and in-fighting that large groups create and would prefer to work with a smaller local group while continuing with my work in Art and teaching. He may have taken that as meaning that I wanted to drop out of his grand designs, but he was unable to write by then, in joined up script at any rate, and due to the brain damage could only print in capitals, so kept in touch via Dr. Sandy MacLennan, a medical and psychiatric doctor living in Inverness, Scotland, who he was consulting for medical advice, and urged me to keep involved. So I just kept my head down and worked as I said with a small East-West, Wiccan-Tantrik, group of four. A good size for a coven, that worked together on a local Common, while I continued to research around the skeleton of Dadaji's system for the Uttarakaulas in the West.

In 2008 a friend of Mike's, living in Oxford, Alex Bennett contacted me and we eventually met at an Alternative Fayre on Midsummer Common in Cambridge, where his mother lived. He became involved with the Fellowship and, being more internet savvy than me, suggested a Facebook group for it, which proved to be a very useful suggestion for expanding interest worldwide. Alex had worked closely with Mike in Oxford on his Indian interests. Mike had become an alternative academic using his Sanskrit and language skills generally, rather than being a practitioner, after his break with Dadaji, and Alex re-introduced us after a break of several years. Unfortunately the two of them had some form of disagreement, Alex eventually lost interest in East-West crossover matters and reverted to Crowley style Thelema. But useful contact with both, but especially Mike again remains, even though that with Alex has dwindled. I am grateful to him for his input.

As a background factor to all of these occurrences it is worth mentioning Kenneth Grant, who set up his own offshoot of Crowley's Order of the Temple of the Orient, the OTO, which became known as the Typhonian OTO, and which Mike would have become head of after Grant's death if Dadaji had not contacted him when an alternative syndicate magazine exchange involved Mike's *'Azoth'* magazine and an Indian magazine called *'Values'* that Dadaji had written articles in crossed over. This caused Mike to travel to India, where he was initiated as an Adi Nath and asked to form a group that became Amookos, and which led him to leave the OTO. Grant had drawn upon all manner of

9

dark mythologies and literary sources to create his Typhonian philosophy linked in his skilful and authoritative sounding writing style, with all the zeal of a reactionary vicar's son, and these had included Tantrika which he did much to popularise amongst occultists. But his general outlook was not one that concurred with Dadaji's, as he had no time for the Quabala or any Middle- Eastern philosophies, let alone any Typhonian constructs, so their letters were few. Dadaji didn't like Crowley being portrayed as "Some kind of sophisticated Satanist" in Grant's *'Aleister Crowley and the Hidden God'*, and famously used a torn up copy of one of Grant's books he had been sent as wrapping paper for a package to send to London. So I began reading Grant more critically after that. The Crowley who Dadaji had known was a Taoist scholar. Later research into Grant's sources have shown them to be very flimsy or bookish not from practice, based on Crowley's contact with David Curwen, who had only done a correspondence course with an Indian sect, The Holy Order of Krishna, that took their inspiration from the Bhagavad Gita, which is central to the Vedic tradition, but has no relation to any of the major indigenous Tantrik traditions. Grant often quotes from *'The Saundarya-Lahari'*, a text about the Sri Vidya Yantra with many spells as a Part Two, to weave into his Typhonian world view, which as a source book is nearer the mark. Another tome of Grant's that talks at length about Tantrika is 'Beyond the Mauve Zone' which was written when he was in contact with Andrew Chumbley, who had had the initial Uttarakaula initiation, without the cult mantra, and done no other work in the tradition, but was telling the world and his uncle that he was to become the next lineage holder, then formed a Tantrik group, Ku Sebbitu, with Michael Staley of the O.T.O., and then his own Ku Trishula or Order of the Negative Trident, of no known members, then dying aged 37. *'Beyond the Mauve Zone'* is peppered with references to the Anuttara Amanaya lineage, which Grant says was the source of information to

Theodore Reuss in his formulation of the original German OTO, never mentioned before, as well as unnamed later contacts. Michael Staley of the Typhonian OTO and myself are of the same opinion that Chumbley was intent on becoming head of that OTO after Grant.

Grant also asked Mike Magee to initiate him into the Adi Nath tradition, but Mike said he knew if he did Grant would take over, so that would never happen while Dadaji was alive. Despite the Adi Nath tradition stemming from Matseyendranath who was prominent in the Kaula tradition which arose out of family, Kula tribal origins, around the Mother Goddess, its direction under Goraksnath led to more of a Shaivite monastic and sadhu phenomenon, and Dadaji's idea to set up grades like Western pseudo-masonic organisations seems more in line with Shaivite orientation. The Uttarakaula side of his legacy is more obviously kaula, where the first three levels of practice are for householders, even though at that stage they can lead to illumination, for either sex, while the remaining planetary rites are largely for sadhus whose family obligations have been discharged and after the cremation ground visions of Aghori have been passed. These rites do lead to siddhi, magical, powers but can be utilised by householders if needs are great enough, and often arise spontaneously. But don't try to run if you have not learned to walk. Sexual rites at any level are about mental Liberation from relative conceptual thought, and Union between Shakti's energy and Siva consciousness. They are not to be confused with Crowley's sex magic which is put to different ends. The Otz Chiim tree of the Quabala, and its roots in Grant's system, are a cosmology for exploring and manipulating the relative phenomenon of the universe, with the possibility of union with the Absolute if the magician persists in his tree climb to the top. Kaula Tantra is about the here and now on Earth, hence the central place of the Goddess who gives life, and Liberation can occur during practice at any stage if conditions are right. There is no hierarchical route to be taken.

Dadaji was of course a sadhu himself, and someone steeped in oral traditions of the Orient. When asked if he could recommend any books, he replied that he "could recommend many for burning", and his guru had told him never to write a book, so he only wrote essays that others have assembled into book form. Similarly what follows is a collection of shorter essays for guidance. Tantrika is not an academic study, although there are many studies about it. It is about practices older than most on the planet, stretching back to the indigenous Indus Valley Civilisation at least.

Once I reached 70 years of age I had to consider how much longer my mortal carcass would be on this planet, so I looked around at the most suitable people I knew to carry on the tradition. There are many good people but I settled on Greg to pass on the responsibilities that Dadaji had given to me as Greg is 20 years younger than me, so both old enough to be experienced in East-West philosophies, but not of an age where he would have only a few years himself to give to the task. It was then Greg's idea that we collect writings from both of us in one volume to make the initiations and inner workings of the Fellowship accessible to a broader audience......and here it is:

John.

Dadaji Mahendranath

Introduction

I first came across John Power's writings when I was travelling in Philadelphia in 2011. I had come to the city to transmit the first inner empowerments of Ordo Sunyata Vajra, an East-West magical group. During one of the groups outings around the city we went to a local bookstore, where I stumbled across *Nu Tantras of the Uttarakaulas* by John Power. Leafing through the pages at the original artwork, and skimming the text, I felt there was a resonance in the material. John had been a devotee of Mahendranath Dadaji, and had been tasked with the job of creating a western transmission of the Uttarakaula (north Indian) line of tantrika. I was intrigued and took it home to read.

Since first encountering the writings of Kenneth Grant in the late 80's, I had felt a strong connection to tantra. Through the hints given in his *Typhonian Trilogies* I began to research and explore, coming into contact with Mike Magee and his wealth of Hindu Tantrik translations. I felt an immediate connection and familiarity with the Goddess Kali, and in these early days I came across a framed photo of her in a small shop in San Francisco, and kept her for many years on my desk.

Tantra, the Goddess, the Sanskrit language, the magical diagrams (yantras) — all of these gave me a thrill unlike anything I had ever encountered before. Early on I received initiation into AMOOKOS and the Adinatha line of Hindu tantra, which gave structure to my studies. Later I would take other tantrik initiations from Hindu and Buddhist lineages. This would culminate in coming into contact with the great Dzogchen master Chogyal Namkhai Norbu, and receiving the direct introduction to the nature of mind. The non-dual realization of Dzogchen continues to be the foundation of my practice, from which tantra radiates out as skilful means, and all of the phenomenal world is an ornamentation of consciousness.

After a nasty divorce, I took the opportunity to start fresh and bought a plane ticket to Nepal. Meditating at the cremation ghats outside Pashupatinath, or sitting in contemplation at the Buddhist shrines, had a magical effect. It was on this trip, while trekking in the Himalayas towards Everest Base Camp, that I had a vivid experience of the Goddess Kali directly.

When I came across John's book, I was freshly back from my Himalayan experiences, and so was struck immediately by his references to both Hindu and Buddhist deities in the material, as well as his own experiences in Nepal, and Pashupatinath in particular.

Dadaji's material had always been very obscure, even opaque to me. It just did not resonate. I knew his history (which John covers in this present book), and his importance originally to the western Uttarakaula tradition, as well as AMOOKOS/Adinatha, but his writings did not resonate for me.

Reading John's book, I noticed his uncanny knack for making sense of the writings of Dadaji. Dadaji is his guru. And this shows in John's writings, with his profound connection and inspiration from the man. Seeing the impact that Dadaji's work had on John's own development and tradition, and the gnosis that John was able to connect with via the tradition that he had taken up from Dadaji. Ultimately it is John's interpretation of Dadaji's work that I find fascinating and of great value.

John and I struck up a rich correspondence and discovered a mutual love of the Goddess, tantra, nature and the Native American cultures. We both had a fondness for Nepal and their blend of Hinduism and Buddhism, as well as the shamanistic history of the land with its connection to the Bon lineages of Tibet. I had performed many tantrik sadhanas at the cremation ghats of Pashupatinath temple in Kathmandu, where John had also travelled and found much inspiration.

We also discovered that we have very different points of view on many core ideas. Where he finds fault in Kenneth Grant, I find profundity and deep inspiration. Where I am critical of Dadaji, John finds a clear path to truth and a real guru. My views on tantra are founded in the traditions of Hindu and Buddhist lineages, whereas John tends to emphasize a type of Vira sadhana of Shiva-Shakti that came from Dadaji.

Nonetheless, or perhaps because of this, we are able to come together and have agreeable disagreements, as well as celebrating our commonalities. And frankly, this is as it should be. Far too often do we find followers and bland rehashing of the same tired information. It is in dialogue and respect for each other's principles that diverse views can come together and move forward.

In this book you will find John's latest thoughts on tantra. In many ways this is an elaboration on what was originally written in *Nu Tantras of the Uttarakaulas*. John has continued to develop his work, and this shows in the latest material. In addition you will also find the unique blend of witchcraft and western paganism that has always been at the core of the western Uttarakauala tradition. This combination makes the western Uttarakaula Fellowship a unique interpretation of a sort of highly westernised Sri Vidya in the context of paganism and wicca.

Here you will find not only the mala and murti, but also the athame and pentacle. Here we find the Hindu goddess Tripurasundari expressing herself as the Goddess of Infinite Space and Infinite Stars, while Ganesh opens and protects the ritual circle along with the spirits of the quarters. Here you will find Dionysian revelry amidst mantras and magick, poetry and art, and perhaps the sounds of a Pan Pipe blowing in the distant forest covered hills, as the rites of the Goddess are celebrated.

ॐ क्रीं   कालिकायै   नम
स्वेच्छाचार

Gregory Peters
Northern California, 2020

Uttarakuru

Dadaji Mahendranath, lineage holder of the Uttarakaulas of India until his death in 1991 often referred to the mystical kingdom of Shambala in his essays, and even named his first Westernised Nath group the Knights of Shambala. Shambala is usually identified as a legendary country hidden in the Himalayas that is most often mentioned in Tibetan Buddhist and Bon literature. It is sometimes passed off as a purely spiritual realm that only the Enlightened can experience, yet at one time it would seem to have had a geographical physicality: Chogyal Namkai Norbu in his researches into Tibetan history, 'Light on Kailash' vol.1 p.24, quotes from an ancient Tibetan manuscript: " To the south of Olmo Lung-ring is Sham-bha-la of India, with Vultures Peak and Bodhgaya". India's border with countries like Nepal has fluctuated over the centuries. Olmo-Ling-ring is itself a legendary Bon realm of the Enlightened, which had an earthly reality and was the birthplace of Tonpa Shenrab, and where he codified and elucidated on the Nine Levels of Bon that evolved out of earlier shamanism. When Buddhism came to Tibet in the 7th Century C.E. Bon was at first sidelined then persecuted and went underground but cross fertilised with Buddhism to create the mode of Tantrik Buddhism known as Vajrayana, until it re-emerged in its own right. Yet the legend of Shambala lived on. The lands of Olmo-Lung-ring lay to the west of Mount Kailash and were said to resemble an eight petalled lotus formed by three rings of mountains. A pyramidal mountain was said to have been at the centre, leading some to associate it with Mount Kailash, which does have a roughly pyramidal form, and four great Indian rivers arise around it. But equally this has been dismissed, as no ruins of the King's palace have been found in the area and the mountain, held in such awe in its own right, has never been climbed. Namkai

Norbu's archaeological explorations in Tibet, published as 'Zhang Zhung, Images from a Lost Kingdom', uphold the alternative notion that Olmo Lung-ring was further to the north-west. Zhang Zhung itself was a larger empire that lasted up to the 8th century C.E., which contained not only Olmo-Lung-ring but all of present Tibet, Nepal, Kashmir Sanscar, parts of Northern India, China up to Karakoram, and even parts of Persia. Mount Kailash was the centre of that empire, and is still sacred to Hindus as Siva and Parvati's abode, as well as of great importance to Bon and Vajrayana Buddhists.

However legends of a Himalayan spiritual paradise on Earth are far more widespread. Buddhists aligned it with ideas they had over legends of a Himalayan spiritual paradise on Earth brought from India. It already existed for them in the Mahabharata, the epic Indian poem that dates back to 8th and 9th centuries, where it was referred to as Uttarakuru. Still the longest poem ever to be written, the Mahabharata relates the history of the Bharati dynasty, including the Princes of the Kuru clan, at the end of the age before the onset of the Kali Age. As we know Uttara is the Indian word for 'north'. Hence Uttarakuru was said to be the realm of the spiritually evolved kingdom of the Northern Kurus. The nomadic tribes of the Asian Steppes that have been named as Scythians had a similar legend, probably relating to the oases of the Tarim Basin. They were an offshoot of the Aryan tribes that invaded India in 2000 B.C.E. when the Indus Valley Civilisation was at its height. Other branches of the Scythians emigrated to become the Celts of Europe. Here we can see Dadaji's use of the 'Rainbow Bridge', imagery linking India and European Paganism. In the Altai Mountains of Siberia the legendary Asian Earthly realm of Enlightened beings is Belovodia. Other hidden valleys of the Himalayas, like Tibetan Khemalung, Nepalese Kyimolung [between Ganesh Himal and Manashu], Sikkim near Mt. Kangchenjunga and Gangtok all have similar legends attached to places only accessible by hidden cave tunnels or forbiddingly dangerous snow covered routes. Interestingly, Kulavadhut, current Lineage Holder of the Uttarakaulas, comes from Gangtok, but modernisation, and an Indian Army presence fearing Chinese encroachment have diminished the area's aura of Earthly paradise. Similarly planes and satellites have failed to reveal signs of hidden spiritual sanctuaries and led to further notions of such places being only available to those possessed of spiritual sight, while pilgrimages searching for these places are seen as analogies for personal self development.

The Mahabharata fed into the literature of the Puranas, whereas the Agamas were of more southerly indigenous Tamil origin and both fed into the literature, from the 9th century onwards, that we refer to as Indian Tantra. But many Bon scriptures that have been preserved or recovered as 'buried spiritual treasures' known as 'terma' in Tibet, are classed as Tantras because of their nature of transformation of the mundane world into a spiritual one , where humans become Gods and Goddesses inhabiting mandalas generated as visualisations with the aid of mantras and other ritual devices. These are plainly far older in the Himalayan regions where invaders did not find the ease of conquest or fertile lands that India offered. Such shamanistic practices fed into the Northern [Uttara] Indian practices as much as Buddhism went in the opposite direction. Similarly Chinese Taoist practices fed in to Indian Tantrika as Chinacara.

When Dadaji asked Pagalababa, his predecessor in the Uttarakaula tradition, where he thought Shambala was, he pointed to his head, his heart, and his cock. So don't pack your snow shoes and ice pick for a pilgrimage just yet: the Tantrik transformation begins right where you are.

Uttarakaula Initiation

At the end of 'Nu Tantras of the Uttarakaulas' I put an appendix entitled Self Initiation, which may have been slightly misleading. It was written at a time when I was making little use of the Internet and was designed to help those seeking initiation after reading the book. It was mainly the text of the Viravrata, the heroic vow, the vow which is taken during the rite, along with details on how to construct the circle to receive the energies transmitted by a member of the Uttarakaula tradition. I did not include the cult mantra. This was only passed on to those actually seeking initiation. Generally the appendix was there to indicate what to expect.

The term 'self initiation' is also in itself misleading. Dadaji and I had corresponded for several years before he asked me to try to make the yoga of the Goddess accessible for Westerners. In 1979 documents arrived to enable me to perform my end of the initiation as he was in India and I was in England. We met several times later, but the international initiation link was the best way to get things underway. This was not a form of initiation that Dadaji had invented, but is dealt with in the 16th arnika of both the 'Tantraloka' and 'Tantrasara' of Abvinavagupta, where he relates how absent initiations can be performed for someone in another country or place, or even post-mortem, as is the case with the 'Tibetan Book of the Dead', or 'Bardo Thodol' as it has been Anglicised, which evolved out of the Bon 'Tantra of the Secret Union of the Sun and Moon' and 'Doctrine of the Six Lights'. By raising the bodily shakti energy in the nadis a net is created that ensnares the soul of the initiate as they are summoned, if recently deceased. For those still living but absent, yet equipped with the information on mandala construction given in the 'Nu Tantras' appendix it is possible in this age of technology for guru and candidate to synchronise the time and ends of their rite, with the initiator preceding his/her actions to those of the candidate's activity. A full Moon at midnight is always chosen.

Most people seeking initiation to the Uttarakaulas will be familiar with other traditions and recognise a dialect of initiations they have undertaken elsewhere. Creation of shrine and circle are the simple beginnings of the first level of activity dedicated to the first aspect of the Goddess as a nubile and morally liberated young woman, Santoshima. For 9 days before Full Moon you can gather what is needed: a raised surface and cloth for a shrine in the East on which is placed a Siva-Shakti yab-yum statue or photo reproduction, a Siva or Vajrayana Buddha for a woman initiate, or a Goddess form for a man [not plastic]. Also a statue or photo of elephant headed God, Ganesh. A photo of the lineage guru, Dadaji, if possible too. All sanctified by incense and salt water, which also reside on the shrine along with cup/glass/chalice for wine, cider or beer [water]; trident or ritual knife [air]; wand of the candidate's devising [fire]; and a plate for ritual offerings [earth]. Food and drink are not part of this rite, but should be offered first to Ganesh, then Siva and the aspect of the Goddess you happen to be working with, then consumed or 'given to the birds'. All the tools need to be censed with incense and marked with salt water too at some point during the 9 days.

On the Full Moon night you can use a length of red wool to mark the circle around your shrine and to give you working space. The rite is performed naked to mark the return to the primordial state. First settle your mind with pranayama deep breathing: in to the count of 9; hold for 4; 9 out, for four cycles. You can count those by fingering a 108 bead mala 'rosary'. Sprinkle the circle with salt water and fume it with incense for three perambulations clockwise. The circle will glow with Light as the circle unfolds and a bindu point above completes a cone or working zonule, as Siva-Shakti yab-yums appear at the cardinal compass points: white East, red South, blue West and green North as you intone

"Om Siva Shakti; Hreem Kreem Kali; Hreem Kleem Lalita; Hreem Tripura Sundari; Om Namah Shivaya. Move the wand to the southern quarter, cup to the west and plate to the north, then " *Om Gam Ganapatai Namah* to Ganesh, and assume meditative position facing East. A chair is possible, if it is fumed and sprinkled. You have created the mandala of Mother-Father archetypes that will come to you in the after life bardos to grant Enlightenment, and remain with your practice throughout life. Ganesh, the elephant headed son of Siva and Parvati guards the underworld. When you start to dream of this mandala you will know that your sadhana [practices] are becoming effective within the deep mind.

At the appointed time use the salt water and incense ash to anoint your brow, heart, navel, genitals, and feet. Then read aloud the Viravrata, and your initiator will have done the same, and made the anointing gestures that you have performed. Also then mark yourself with a downward pointing triangle from right shoulder to pubes to left shoulder, with the words Peace, Freedom, Happiness, read the last verse of the Viravrata and vibrate the cult mantra that has been given to you. Rest in meditation of what has taken place, then as formless a meditation as you can manage, while continuing pranayama.

To close the rite reverse what you did to open it: returning ritual tools to the shrine then, as the Light unwinds anti-clockwise three revolutions back to earth, while the ritual energy returns to the bindu point above. Facing the shrine thank the Goddess in her form as Santoshi Ma for helping you to complete the rite, stamp your left then right foot on the floor and perform the Taoist Arch of the back with heels raised so that feet chakras in the bawls complete the grounding. You have completed during the preparation and execution of the rite the work of the first level of shrine and circle, which you can repeat until you wish to move on to the second level. Practice empty mind meditation, so that thoughts pass by without attachment viewed like a stream, and you are open to receive the ecstatic energy of the second level. Begin to keep a dream and inspirational diary, if you don't already.

At the second level the aspect of the Goddess[Lalita] Shanti presides for the ruler, the Moon and when your circumstances provide the opportunity maithuna ecstatic sexual union practice can proceed. You are in a position to initiate your partner if they wish by reversing the polarities to self and deity which you used in your own initiation. If they do not wish to take initiation you can still benefit from their sexual polarity to yours during normal sexual relations but will have to do so only by mental visualisations and involve no ritual paraphenalia. As a man you would mentally construct your cone of power during foreplay and assume the Godform of Siva with the mantras *Om Namah Shivaya* and *Sivohim* and invoke the Goddess into your partner with *Hreem Kleem Lalita Shanti*. If female use *Om Namah Shivaya* only to invoke Siva into your partners aura. You have the four elements in your circle, prolonged ecstatic sex is the quintessence which is the engine of shakti energy and needs lasting psycho-physical connection of the polarised bodies to reverse the female energy into a downward flow from crown to vagina, which rises in the male up to the crown. Until the woman has begun to orgasm this cannot happen and premature ejaculation will have to be mixed with interludes of oral sex to revive the phoenix. The 5 'm' elements written of in many books on Tantrika [Hindu words beginning with m for meat, fish cereal, wine and sex] are elements of ritual usually used in Siva cults but in Kaula Goddess cults other symbols of the elements can be used, cannabis, smoked or as a bhang drink, for [cereal] earth for instance and vegetable foods instead of meat and fish. Meat is the male lingam and fish vaginal secretions of the shakti. The food and drink feast prelude can be as elaborate or simple as chosen, but indigestion is not going to improve the yoga. Changes to consciousness are more likely to be *as a result of* the ritual rather than *during* it. Prevention of orgasm by men as in Vajrayana Buddhism is an old Pisces-Virgo Age formula not suitable to the present day. Otherwise the sex rites of the second level are continuous for householders. Midnight and full moon continue to be favoured for these rites. Nightly practice will soon lead to exhaustion and everyday sexual relations can remain as normal.

Kenneth Grant did manage to popularise knowledge of the movement of the kalas in the female organism in his writings, but in characteristically egocentric manner he associated it with using control of female genital secretions in degenerate ways to create elixir for longevity in what is nothing more than vampirism. His sources were not from enlightened practitioners in the 5 great Tantrik schools but from interlopers who had sought to use practices from within tantrik sadhana devoid of grounding in any of the 5 directional traditions of Tantrika and for singular debased use only. No success to use of these thefts was ever reported. Exchange of fluids by partners is health giving. Robbing others of them for personal ends is not, and only creates bad karma.

A kala is a measure of time and the female organism secretes hormones and varying fluids into discharge at different times of the month in a circular fashion from different erogenous zones around the body which can be stimulated by acupressure in foreplay to enhance the constituents of secretion. Beginning at full Moon shakti energy can be found to be most powerful in the forehead chakra, but following the nadis other than the sushuma it descends with the waning Moon down the left side of the body via eyes, cheeks, lips, chin, neck, shoulder, armpit, breast, side, hip, pubic region, genitals, thigh, knee, shin, and ankle to the foot chakras and is grounded at the dark of the Moon. At new Moon it begins its ascent up the right side of the body. The circular motion is characteristically centripetal female in motion, while male energy is centrifugal and uses the sushuma to aim for the full moon energy and to clear the chakras of knots. Skilful art can employ this knowledge and technique to enhance lovemaking during foreplay, as months evolve. Not only hands but feet also can be used to stimulate acupressure points, as well as the mouth and tongue while kissing or for clitoral stimulation. The crossing points of lines on the Sri Yantra have been identified with bodily centres mentioned above by some people, so stimulation of the 14 marma points and chakra regions can be seen to stimulate the flow into the genital outlet to conform with the yantra's sensitive points. This happens with or without reference to the yantra but gives an explanation of its form. The body is real and the yantra a diagram. The Moon mantra to stop the mind from wandering and also to stimulate nectar flow is *Oang soong Somaya namha.*

The third level comes under the aspect of the Goddess [Lalita] Tripura and involves the study and use in rites of Yantras and Mantras especially the Sri Yantra. In 'Nu Tantras' I gave this as the meditation extended into the 3D zonule with Siva mantras to cleanse the chakras, but to invoke the Goddess Lalita Tripura into the zonule, and possibly your partner, or self if female, for rites the mantra is *Ka e i la hreem ha sa ka ha la hreem sa ka la hreem shreem.* There are variations on this, but if you want to be in the zonule with, or as, Lalita for your sex rites you have the means. The planetary correspondence is Jupiter.

The fourth level takes the aspirant into the first abyss with the aspect of the Goddess Aghori and Saturn as ruler. Graveyards become a suitable place to conduct rites, or when your circle can be bedecked with Saturnian symbols in contemplation of the impermanence of life. This stage marks the move to that of the Sadhu, the holy dropout beyond the life of the householder and aspiring to complete moksha: union with the Absolute and liberation from the rounds of rebirth. Other levels produce siddhi , magical powers which are too intrusive and time consuming to go with the household life. The levels are not hierarchic like the quabala. Realisation can come whilst at householder levels. Tantrika is of the Goddess and for her created world, not to escape from it. Sadhus are usually men, but sometimes widows. Women bring us into the world and usually dominate household life even if they work outside to help maintain households. Saturnian mantras include *Oang eang haring shring sani charya namaha* and *Dhoong Dhoong Dhumavati tha tha* and the yantra is a six pointed star in an 8 petalled lotus within the 4 gates, for anyone thinking of moving into this life phase, and beyond.

The Mahavidyas or Wisdom Goddesses

From most published sources about the Wisdom Goddesses of India, or more correctly, *aspects* of the Goddess, it would be easy to assume that there were ten fixed forms of the deity. But this has not been, and is not always, so. All dialects of Goddess worship are ultimately traceable to Kali, who was known as far back as the Indus Valley civilisation, prior to the Aryan conquest. Together with the Horned Lord of the Beasts, Pashupatinath, an early form of Siva, Kali can be referred to as one of the pair of primordial deities. Celts, who arose from the Steppes of Asia Minor almost certainly brought the couple to Europe as Kernunnos and his Consort. Both variations of the couple are worshipped at crossroads: mandalas where forces in the landscape meet as the genius loci, or spirits of place.

A later development comes in the form of Lalita, Sri or Tripura whose main focus for worship and yoga is with the Sri Yantra magick diagram by those known as Sri Kulas. Lalita is said to have emerged from the union of Mahakala [Siva] and Adyar [Kali] in supreme bliss. Her many forms include Lalita, Mahatripura Sundari, or Sodasi, Tripura Bhairavi, Bhuvanesvari, Bala Tripura Sundari and Rajarajesvari. Her worship is through Sri Vidya Yantra and Mantra. The Sri Kulas also connect Matangi, Bagala or Kamala to Sri Vidya practice. The earliest found scriptural reference to the Sri Yantra have been found dating to the 7th century C.E. and oddly, come from Indonesia. No detailed texts on Sri Vidya have been found in India before the 13th century.

An early systematisation of the aspects of the Goddess can be found in the Epic Mahabharata, from the 6th century C.E., after Aryan additions to the Hindu pantheon. These are seven in number and known as the Matrikas, or Mothers of the Saptamatrika. A temple in South India devoted to the Saptamatrika pre-dates the Mahabharata histories by a century, to the 5th. The seven Matrikas are six Devi Shaktis of Hindu Gods and the seventh is Kalika Chamunda- the essence of the Devi herself- so back to Kali again.

The best known form of the Ten Mahavidyas emerged in the 12th century, after Tara was added from Himalayan origins. They fall into two sub groups: the Kali Kula group of Kali, Tara, Chinnamasta and Dhumavati, and the Sri Kula group of Sundari [Sodasi/Lalita], Bhuvanesvari, Tripura Bhairavi, Matangi, Bagala and Kamala [Laksmi]. When Dadaji codified the aspects of the Goddess for Westerners he identified nine, and did not include Tara. Although some of the names of the Goddesses mentioned above do appear in his rendition of the aspects, some appear to have been given a personal dialect, as for instance when he used a name that had been revived and used as the name for a liberated modern Indian woman in a 20th century Bollywood film. Nine is also a number sacred to Shambala, spiritual centre of the ancient Zhang-Zhung empire of Tibet, Nepal, Kashmir, and parts of China and North India and even parts of Persia. The first king of Tibet was crowned on a throne of nine steps to symbolise the nine levels of Bon practice. The Chinacara aspect that Dadaji brought to light in the Uttarakaula, North Indian, tradition of Tantrika can also be seen in the use of the Sino-Tibetan I Ching and in Taoist dialects of sex magick. The aspects of the Goddess enumerated by Dadaji were Santoshima, Shanti, Tripura, Aghori, Digambari, Kali, Ambika, Durga and Lalita. Each is associated with planetary and other correspondences in order to construct appropriate rituals. Because practitioners are predominantly householders the first three grades are the most important basis of continued practice and realisation can occur at any time during this. As such it is the inverse of the hierarchies of the Western Quabala, where grades higher up the tree are given greater importance. After the forth Uttara level of practices practitioners are moving into the realms of the Sadhus with spontaneous manifestation of siddhis [magic powers] that develop given in the time devoted to the holy dropout lifestyle of practice.

Also in the Uttara tradition there is another Goddess system of aspects based solely on Kali, known as Prabhakali, or the wheel of the twelve rays of Light of Kali: the Kali of Creation, the Kali of Persistence, the Kali of Destruction, the Kali of Passion, the Good Kali, the Kali of Control, the Kali of Death, Auspicious Kali, the Kali of the Supreme Sun, the Terrible Kali, and the Great Kali. In the age of Pisces/Virgo Kumari the virgin pre-menstrual Goddess presided at the centre of the circle as the 13th deity. Kumari is also an important deity in Nepal, where she is part of an eightfold group of Goddesses, called the Asta Martikas: Rudrani, Brahmyani, Vaishnavi, Indrani, Chamunda Varani, Mahakakshmi, and Kumari. The virgin archetpe was revered in most traditions in the Age of Pisces/Virgo.

So not just ten Mahavidyas then , but 7, 8, 9, 10, 12 or 13, in two main streams of Kali or Lalita. All ultimately resolve into Kali. It doesn't matter which system you chose, but obviously in the tradition descending from Dadaji we use the nine-fold aspects that he enumerated.

Background of the Uttara Mahavidyas

Anyone who has seen 'Nu Tantras of the Uttarakaulas' will have realised that in committing images of the aspects of the Goddess to canvas that Dadaji had identified by choice or inheritance, that I used the Tantrik technique of Transformation, by casting partners at different times into the roles. Here I would like to expand on the traditional qualities of the Goddesses that informed those transformations, minus multiple limbs and associated symbols that evolved in Indian iconography, and that I deemed inappropriate for Western minds:

Santoshi Ma: young mother of satisfaction, is a daughter of Ganesh and one of his consorts who originated in the Nepal and North India. She was revived by Bollywood in a film in 1960 called 'Jai Santoshi Maa' as embodiment of a liberated young woman. There may also be a connection to one of the 9 Nath incarnations: Santoshnath, an incarnation of Vishnu, who took the name after performing tapas and austerities.

Shanti Devi: is a Goddess of Peace, who fed into Hinduism from Jainism. She is worshipped at midnight during Full Moon, and Fridays are also auspicious for her puja.

Tripura: the triple Goddess Lalita Tripura, waxing, full and waning to Kali aspect. She is associated with Sri Vidya and is also known as Sodashi Devi, where she appears in other groupings of Mahavidyas.

Aghori: is *not dreadful* even though she is the dweller of the cremation ground. She encourages us to look beyond distinctions of life and death in impermanence and underlying reality.

Digambari: the sky clad Goddess, again fed into the Hindu melting pot from Jain origins.
She is associated with Saraswati and Matangi. Jains favoured nudity and it survived for women longest in rural Kerala, South India despite invading missionary censorship. A tax was even imposed on Dalit women based on the size of breasts! But one Keralan woman, Nangeli, cut her breasts off and bled to death in front of the tax collector. Her husband reversed the Suti ritual and jumped on her funeral pyre. Only then was the tax abandoned.

Kali: the primeval black Goddess whose origins can be traced back as far as the oldest known Indian civilisation in the Indus Valley. She is adopted into the [Aryan] Mahabharata epic poem, of around the 6th century, as a wrathful black Goddess. O.K. if you keep her wrathfulness on your side!

Ambika: was born of Parvati and is also known as Kansiki, which means 'black'. Like Durga she was created as a demon slayer: 'a black maiden with a lustre of a thundercloud'. When Parvati retired to the Himalayas Ambika evolved into the Sattvic aspect of Parvati as guardian of the household and model of motherhood. She is mentioned in the 'Devi Mahatmya', of the 6th Century, and the 'Siva Purana'.

Durga is well known in Hinduism, but her origins are as a Himalayan folk Goddess and vegetation Goddess. She was one of the Septamatrikas by 500 B.C.E. She was adopted into the Mahabharata and she also appears in the Tamil Puranas too. She was created to kill demons that other Gods could not destroy. She was a shakti of Siva at one stage of her evolution but became independent, as in, for example, the 'Naryan Upanishad' of the 7th and 8th centuries.

Lalita, is the young woman, innocent as the new Moon, of the Tripura triad and presides over the Sri Yantra and its spells as well as the Ultimate transcendence of shakti power with Siva consciousness.

Mantras for puja and evocation are best constructed with name and suitable bijas and personal native languages for Westerners, if you don't want to spend all your time memorising Indian tongue twisters.

The Triads of the Goddess's Aspects

Santoshima: presides over basic shrine practice and circle
casting.

Shanti Devi: presides over polarity and sex magick
experiments.

Tripura: presides over yantras, especially the Sri
Yantra.

***

Aghori: mantra, yantra; mediumship; the after
death bardos. The first Abyss.

Digambari: Earth magick, ley lines; elementals and
directional guardians; art,music, poetry,
drama.

Kali: the magick of the chrone; auto eroticism, kalas,
acupressure; herbs and potions. The second
Abyss.

***

Ambika: mantra and yantra again; sigilisation; oracles;
astrology.

Durga: martial arts and protection magick.

Lalita: erotic magick of Light. Anuttara empty mind
consciousness. Gifts of siddhi.

34

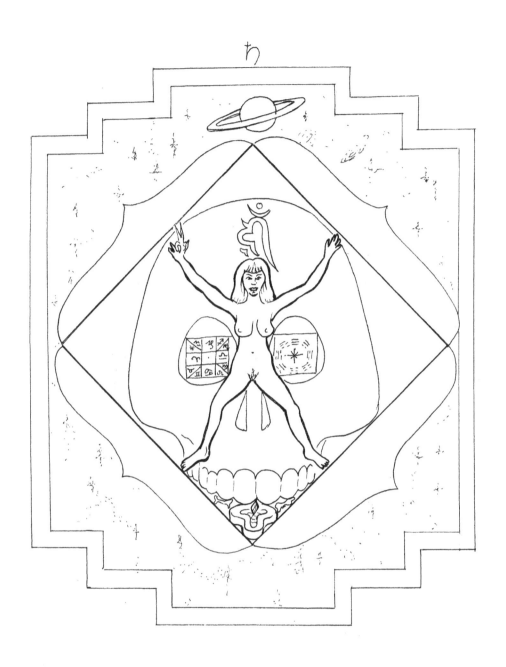

38

41

Pranayama

"Select a zonule and sit [with spine] upright, comfortable and relaxed. No mechanical contrivances or plastic objets d'art are needed. The posture itself is the expression of the simple and easy. Keep the mind awake or you will have strayed into failure. Trance, unconsciousness and sleep are all instruments of defeat.

"In the preliminary and early exploratory mind wanderings concentrate by counting [on a mala of beads] and much rhythmic breathing:
Count the breath as it goes in and out: seven in, hold for four, breath out, hold, repeatedly.

" Pranayama means holding the breath between breathing in and breathing out for the period of four or five heartbeats. Indian saints teach that prana is identical and synonymous with the Supreme Substance, and holding the breath absorbs it. Thus is expounded the secret of pranayama and its power, for this creates environmental conditions for realisation."

Dadaji Mahendranath.

There are many prescribed materials for malas, but most will be difficult to source outside of India, except maybe coral, which is favoured for Goddess puja. Rudrakshas are favoured by Kali and Lalita and bone by Aghori. Rudrakshas can sometimes be found in import shops, but would have to be the small berries for 108 length. 50s are sometimes used. Plastic is a no-no but wood or other natural materials are the best of more easily obtainable ones. Indian Tantra as we know it flourished in the Piscean Age, even though much of it was a reaction to Vedic norms. A lot of ritual paraphernalia bears the mark of elaborate Piscean glamours, but practice remains simple, and intention is more important than outward show of offering. Pranayama breathing is is of course linked to meditation and mantra can also be used to time sequences of breathing.

Prana is not to be seen just as oxygenation of the body but rather as the fuel that powers the bodily alchemy of transformation. Polluted air will do more harm than good and natural open spaces or well ventilated interiors are essential as places of practice.

Various authorities have prescribed different regimes of breathing for pranayama, such as 7 in, hold for 1, 7 out, hold for 1, which is little more than normal deep breathing. Dadaji, above, puts the emphasis on holding the breath, so 7 in, 4 hold, 7 out, 4 hold, as being a more effective means of absorbing prana. This can be extended to 9 in, hold 5, 9 out, 5 hold, with practice as the downward breath reaches further down to stir the shakti energy stored at the base of the spine. Over the first ten weeks once practice has commenced use the 7-4 regime for 12 cycles; after that use the cycle twice daily for another ten weeks; then raise it to 15 minutes twice a day. For use during coitus both partners need to be able to maintain the cycle for 30 minutes and eventually up to an hour, during which time electrical and magnetic energies will cross over between partners to create shared circuits that stimulate the energies in the basal region to activate higher centres. Dadaji called his slant on practices Twilight Yoga. That is because the best times to practice are the liminal points of the day: dawn/after waking, noon, evening twilight, and midnight. It is not good to practice on a full stomach, when ill, tired, or after strenuous exercise. Similarly the yearly liminal seasons of Spring and Autumn are good times to begin practice, and then on the new Moon.

During normal breathing we do not stop to consider that our breath moves in a cycle between nostrils, in periods of 20 to 25 minutes through each in turn, with change-overs when the breathing is through both nostrils simultaneously. The left nostril carries the magnetic 'lunar' or ida current, while the right nostril carries the positively charged electric 'solar' or pingala current. The central balanced sushuma is fed by both channels. Our bodies are symmetrical and these three currents make their cycle in the spinal chord energising throat, lungs, heart, solar plexus, and ovaries in women or testicles of men before culminating in the basal centre and going on to energise knee, ankle and grounding centres before returning and rising to the brow and crown. 'Knots' of energy form at crossover points around the endocrine glands which the sushuma energy equalises through pranayama, allowing for free flow. The ida 'Moon' breath feeds the sympathetic nervous system, while the pingala 'Solar' breath feeds the vasomotor system of virility and activity. Psychic faculties are stimulated when the balanced sushuma breath energy is flowing, but it is also a time when fateful life events can take place, and psychic attacks are most effective if not protected against.

It is said that during conception that if a man's breath is in the solar nostril flow and the mother's breath through the lunar nostril a boy will result. If conversely the man's breath is in the lunar nostril, while the mother's is in the solar nostril they will have a girl child. If mother and father are both breathing in solar or lunar flow a homosexual child will result. Although the symbolic implications would seem to fit there has been no statistical evidence to confirm this as parents are usually otherwise preoccupied to be observing which nostril they are breathing in!

When wishing to stimulate solar flow for dynamic outgoing, or conversely lunar flow for passive activities like Art or gardening, the required flow can be achieved by lying on the side opposite to the nostril with head propped by the arm , while giving pressure to the armpit with the opposite hand will also stimulate the changeover. Massaging the big toe of the opposite foot is yet another method. Perhaps the simplest but short term method is to block the nostril taking in the unwanted breath. For Sadhus it is said that lunar flow all day and solar flow at night is the optimum flow of breath, when a more balanced flow would seem natural. But for the householder with all the preoccupations that daily life entails the normal balanced interchange is certainly the only option.

It is interesting to note that the Chinese have the channels that Indians call ida and pingala running down the front and back of the body, not left and right of sushuma!

Marmas

In 'The Tantra of Blowing the Mind' Dadaji says, when talking of the chakras, that there are many more throughout the body, and mentions ones in the hands for healing. There is similarly one in each of the bawls of the feet, where nerves to the toes cross tendons, which are used for grounding. These are part of the bodily centres referred to as marmas, rather than chakras. Like the example of the foot given above they occur at junctions [*sandhis*] of anatomical structures like nerves, muscles, bones, joints and internal organs. They are akin to acupuncture points, although fewer in number, and require less precision in locating the points. They are activated by acupressure, rather than needles, herbs or massage for therapeutic purposes and sexual arousal, if you choose the correct ones, so form a very important part in foreplay leading to ecstasy. This is tied into the monthly movements of the kalas in women. The energy flow from the endrocrine glands, which are the outer functioning of the chakras, thus stimulated and flowing out of the nadi branches from chakras and marma points is called *ojas* and give strength to the immune system. At the other end of the scale some marma centres are used as attack points in martial arts. So great care in the manipulation of marmas is needed, and they are best studied under guidance from someone with practical knowledge of the use of Ayurvedic medicine.

Apart from the chakras related to the endrocrine glands, yogic introspection has identified 14 other channels that carry energies

46

around the body. Foremost of these are ida and pingala, the two snake-like channels that appear weaving around the central spinal nadi, the sushuma, and its chakra centres symbolised in Western cultures as the Caduceus rod of Mercury. They distribute the energy from breathing [prana]. The other major centres serve the limbs and their joint centres where the marmas are located, and can be stimulated by acupressure, especially in women as the kala energies of hormones and other bodily elements that comprise them follow their monthly circuit of bodily and limb centres, which obviously play a great part in the creative forces of childbirth. They reach their zenith at the top of the head at full Moon, move down the right of the body until they are in the genital area at the dark of the Moon, and return up the left side of the body. They are at maximum strength as elixir just before the half circuit is complete, 10-14 days into the cycle, but Full Moon is best for transcendental maithuna. After an hour's contact and coition the prana currents reverse direction down the female body and up the male sushuma instead of the procreation direction of down the male to receptive female. The supreme secret of yab-yum coition is that the female has to bring her skakti energy from the Sahasrara level down the sushuma to her muladhara to begin the flow up the male's centres for it to rise and complete the interlocked circuit. Where nadis and muladhara meet at the root chakra prana arrives to regulate eliminatory functions, then moves on to the svadisthana chakra to stimulate sexual arousal. Lack of such stimulation will lead to poor health and low oja energy levels.

The Ananga-Ranga, Indian Medieval love manual, only gives the above case, but recent science has shown women can enter the 28 day solar energy emission cycle at any stage and this has a knock on effect through life, so individual experiment is necessary to establish the relation to the cycle.

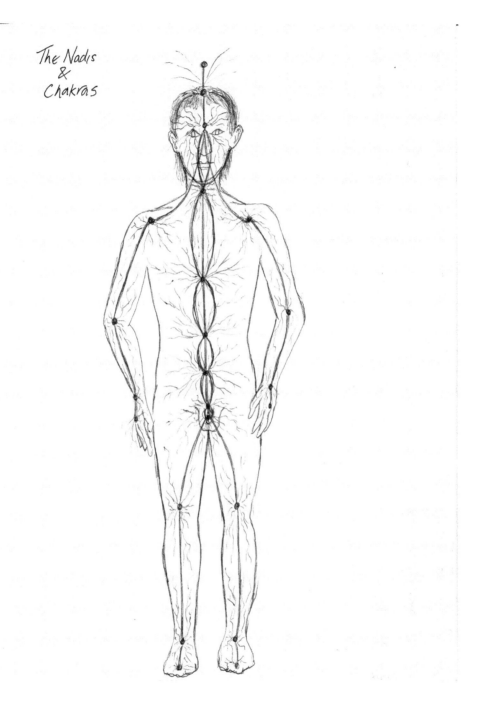

The Nadis
&
Chakras

Shakta Bija Mantras

Bija means seed, and so bija Mantras are the core sounds around which longer mantras are built. On their own 108 repetitions are needed to make them effective. The 'Meru Tantra' anticipated a time when when bija mantras would be incorporated in longer forms of mantra using languages other than Sanskrit. For Kaulas to know how to construct longer mixed language mantras it is necessary to know the effects of the building blocks that are the bijas:

Aum energises prana for ojas from the chakras

Hreem is for solar energy currents

Shreem is for lunar energy currents

Kreem, associated with Kali, transmits electrical energy

Kleem, associated with Lalita is magnetic, so attractive, energy

Hum,[Hoom] is transformative fire of Siva

Haum is also a Siva mantra and revitalises by giving energy to prana

Streem brings expansion and is associated with Durga

Dum is another Durga mantra and is used for protection, like

Phat, which clears unwanted forces from ritual spaces

Treem, transcends difficulties and is associated with Tara

Saum balances solar and lunar energies of the nadis

Sauh causes nectar to flow from the crown chakra

Hleem and Swaha are endings to mantra chains.

Single letters of the Sanskrit alphabet, or their equivalents can also be used to build up mantras along with bijas. The most important of these for Shaktas is that used with the Sri Yantra to invoke the Goddess Tripura Sundari:

Ka E I La Hreem

Ha Sa Ka La Hreem

Sa Ka La Hreem.

There are variations on this.

Planetary Mantras

For use in constructing rituals beyond, and in addition to, the first three Householder levels.

	Seed	Full
Sun	Hreem	Aim Hraam Hreem Hraum
Sar Suryaya namah		
Moon	Shreem	Aim Shraam Shreem
Sraum Sah Candraya namah		
Jupiter	Greem	Aim Graam Greem Graum
Sah Gurave namah		
Saturn	Priim	Aim Praam Priim Praum
Sah Sanaye namah		
Mercury	Briim	Aim Braam Briim Braum
Sah Budhaya namah		
Venus	Driim	Aim Draam Driim Draum
Sah Sukraya namah		
Uranus		
Mars	Kreem	Aim Kraam Kreem Kraum
Sah Kujaya namah		
Neptune		

There are no mantras given for Uranus and Neptune as they are not used in Indian Astrology but
the mantras for Rahu [North extremity of the Moon's orbit] and Ketu [South extremity] can be used for Neptune and Uranus respectively as they are similar in natures, but shouldn't be used if the rituals have relevance to planetary position movements listed in ephemerides. Ephemerides are otherwise used to find beneficial times to perform planetary rites. For weekdays rituals use Sun: Sunday, Moon: Monday, Mars: Tuesday, Mercury: Weds., Jupiter: Thurs., Venus: Fri, Saturn: Sat., Rahu/ Neptune,Thurs., Ketu/ Uranus: Saturday. All 108 repetitions on your mala.

Neptune [Rahu]   Bhreem   Aim Bhraam Bhreem Bhraum Sah Neptunave namah

Uranus [Ketu]   Streem   Aim Straam Streem Straum Sah Uuranave namah

Using mantras for planets beyond Saturn is an issue that highlights the difference between Indian, sidereal astrology and Western placings of planets in the zodiac's pre-precession positions, because India has not admitted the more recently discovered planets into calculations, despite updating the zodiac to precessional astronomical position. So if the Rahu and Ketu mantras do not seem a convincing usage, as this group is East-West fusion in essence, then some may feel more comfortable using Western words of power, or using the Indian Jupiter mantra, above, for Neptune and Saturn mantra for Uranus, as these are attributions of the new planets as additional rulers of zodiacal signs Pisces and Aquarius in Western Astrology.

Birth Chart Decoder:
[If someone has done your natal chart]:

First look at the whole: if more planets are above the horizon the native is an Extrovert, if below an Introvert. If most planets are on the rising half of the chart [left side] then the first half of life will be best for self expression; if setting [right side] then the second half of life will be better.

Rising sign or 'ascendant' [that shown on the mid left], Sun sign, and Moon sign [the zodiacal signs these' planets' are in] are the strongest factors. **Study planets qualities first then how they are affected by the qualities of signs and houses they fall in, and what aspects [angles to other planets they make.]** If time of day of birth is not known then the ascendant can't be established, nor the 12 Houses that follow on from it, so only a partial chart can be done.

Conjunctions and oppositions of planets are also strong indicators and the effect is judged by the qualities of the planet [see below], and what zodiacal sign and House they are in [also below].

Count how many planets are in fire signs Aries, Leo, and Sagittarius, for energy, how many in air signs Aquarius, Gemini, and Libra, for intellect, how many are in water signs Pisces, Cancer and Scorpio for emotion; and in Earth signs Taurus, Virgo and Capricorn for practicality. And see which predominate.

Abbreviations and traditional Meanings :

Asc: Ascendant, the sign rising at birth : your persona- how others see you.

Desc: Descendant, the sign setting at birth: partnerships, marriage, others, potential enemies.

M/c: medium coeli or midheaven : career [10th house]: philosophy or religion [9th house]. Mother.

I/c: immunum coeli or nadir : home [4th house] local travel [3rd house]. Father.

Planets:

Sun: Power, vitality, self, expression.

Moon: Responsiveness, instinct, fluctuation.

Mercury: Mental and physical communication.

Venus: Harmoniousness, sex and pleasure, Arts.

Mars: Energy, initiative, conflict: aggression or protection.

Jupiter: Expansion, rulership, wealth, philosophy.

Saturn: Limitation, hard work, old age, suffering, death.

Uranus: Inventiveness, revolution, eccentricity, sudden disruptive change.

Neptune: Nebulous, mystical, drink, drugs.

Pluto: Elimination, executive action, big business, wealth, underworld.

Zodical Signs and Houses :

Aries   and 1st House: Self, assertiveness, energy, urgency.

Taurus   and 2nd House: Money pleasure, steadfastness, possessiveness.

Gemini   and 3rd House: Local travel, communication [writing, techno etc.], learning, versatility.

Cancer   and 4th House: Home, nurturing and protecting, sensitivity.

Leo   and 5th House: Children, creativity, vitality, energy, power, humour, drama.

Virgo   and 6th House: Health, work, critical and analytical ability.

Libra   and 7th House: Partnerships, judgement, sense of fair play, balance, harmony.

Scorpio   and 8th House: Executive capabilities, death afterlife, underworld.

Sagittarius and 9th House: Wisdom, emancipation, philosophy, long distance travel, exploration.

Capricorn   and 10th House: Work, career, aspiration.

Aquarius   and 11th House: Independence, humanity, originality, eccentricity.

Pisces   and 12th House: Nebulous mysticism, impressionability, outward show, glamour.

Aspects [Angles between Planets.]

Conjunction [up to 8 degrees]   strong points in a chart.

Opposition   [near180   degrees   by   8   degrees] conflicting factors.

Square [near 90 degrees by 8 degrees]   slowing but often stabilising.

Trine [near 120degrees by 8 degrees]   helpful, positive influence.

   Moderate and Weak aspects:

Sextile[within 5 degrees of 60] moderate positive influence.

  Sesquiquadrate [within 2 degrees of 135]

Quincunx [within 2 degrees of 150]

Semi Square [within 2 degrees of 45]

Semi sextile [within 2 degrees of 30.

*

Not planets, but the highest and lowest points of the Moon's orbit, the Dragon's Head   [top] and Dragon's Tail   [bottom] are also placed in the zodiac for the time of birth and show, Head, the beginnings of cycles and, Tail, endings of cycles, according to position in the zodiac.

*

The zodiac appears to move by 30 degrees as seen from earth every 2000 years, in what is called precession, so the astronomers zodiac is not the astrologers. The former is referred to as the sidereal zodiac, and is the one used in most oriental schools of astrology. My experience is that the meanings attached to parts of the sky over the last 2000years remain with them and astrology has to address this issue as precession continues.

By referring to an ephemeris [tables of planetary movement] and comparing it to birth position you can see when it is and isn't a good time for certain activities. It won't tell you what WILL happen in the future!

Yantras

Yantras are visual equivalents of the energies aroused by mantra. They can be used as foci for meditation or pro-active ritual according to the energies they represent, used as sigils for these purposes, or internalised by installing them on the body or using them as three dimensional cones dedicated as spaces to work within.

There is scant evidence of how the geometric meditation devices that we refer to as yantras evolved. One image carved on stone found near Allahabad in Uttara Pradesh shows triangular motifs and Goddess figures and has been dated to 20,000 years B.C.E. Whether it is realistic to cite such finds as ancestors of yantras could be seen as far fetched. Their relevance to the history of yantras rests only on whether they originated before the Aryan invasion of India. If rudimentary yantras were employed by the indigenous natives, or if they arrived with the Aryan tribes, will never be clear. Certainly the reactions to the Aryan occupations that gave rise to Tantrika could not claim with any certainty that they were of Tamil or Indus Valley origin, and seem to have been employed in Vedic ritual in some form from early on. There is no evidence that yantras were imported from Tibetan Bon practice or that of neighbouring countries. Rather it seems that they were taken North when Buddhism moved there and morphed with Bon to create Vajrayana. Their use in Tantrik ritual can be easily shown in the Golden Age of Indian Tantrika in the 8th and 9th centuries C.E. But before that there was common usage in both streams of Indian Civilisation. Worldwide they may simply have evolved in various dialects from the basic magic circle around the crossroads, of gathering points. They certainly would have appealed to Tantrik practitioners as they are seen as instruments of transformation through visualisation. They present a visual equivalent to the sound vibrations of mantrik repetition in fixing the mind to single areas of consciousness identified as Gods, Goddesses or planetary influences. Whatever the case it seems that they will have evolved as ideograms of natural forces encountered by, and represented by, natives in the same way that the symbols used in the letters of language, Matrikas, arose.

Yantras are often found on the ground plans of temples, and even mark out the ground plans of these buildings. Meditation mats often bear yantra patterns and both these uses are a clue to their major function which is often overlooked by Westerners who are used to seeing them as flat surfaces in book reproductions or on posters. But in meditation and magic they are 3 dimensional cones or working zonules, like the cones of power employed by European Witches, that have all been reduced to flat surfaces for reproduction. They do have a function in a flat form however when they are drawn as sigils for talismans, but for meditation and magic ritual operations the participants sit and act within the visualised mental constructs of the zonule to practice the deep rhythmic breathing that is pranayama, sometimes performing ritual actions like mudra, where energies are said to be installed upon the body. The simplest of these being blessing of the chakra regions.

The elements that make up most yantras are:

the point: bindu, the first emergence of manifestation as a seed;

the straight line: as the point moves it creates a line;

the circle: when centrifugal forces are restrained by centripetal forces it takes the form of a circle, which the Ancients observed in nature's cycles everywhere;

the cross: when the centre point expands to the compass directions and male, vertical meets female, horizontal it creates the four elements, while the central bindu point is the quintessence;

the swastika: when the elements begin to revolve the four branches leave energy tails that form the swastika. This usually follows the Sun's direction, referred to as the right hand path, but revolving anti Sunwise the left hand path is the sensual path that reverses societal norms. Which way galaxies swirl varies according on you viewpoint in space;

the triangle: pointing upwards this denotes fire, like a flame, and the male principle, while when the point is downwards it is like water and falling raindrops. It also recalls the female pubic triangle which also has downward motion in relation the manifestation of childbirth;

the hexagram: where male flame and female droplet unite;

the hourglass of triangles: when male and female separate until they only touch at one point, this leads to dissolution and the end of once creative cycles. This the form that Siva's drum, the damaru, takes as the sands of time run out;

the pentagram: five joined triangles of fire, with a pentagon inside representing air. It is called 'the remover of desire', 'conqueror of obstacles', and is for protection. In another form found in yantras five equilateral triangles are placed alternatively, point uppermost and then point below, inside one another. Point uppermost in the largest triangle denotes Siva; point below in largest triangle denotes a Goddess. The usual form of pentagram but with two points uppermost is a symbol of Siva Pashupatinath, and procreation.

the square: is the earth element and building blocks;

lotuses: made of curving lines represent watery elements. Different numbers of petals in further circles beyond the usual eight directional lotus are used to stress the importance of certain deities [usually 16 secondary petals] and in chakra yantras also vary in their numbers of petals.

As well as the temple yantras and meditation mats already mentioned we could also mention other applications such as
foundation yantras, under seats, under houses and temples,

mandala yantras at the centre of group practice,

chakra yantras for each of the bodily centres that function through the endrocrine glands:
these are visualised as flat patterns with Sanskrit letters on them and used to focus on individual energies for specific purposes. They are of course artistic creations, and talk of the number of petals for each are part of these aids for concentration, but are mental constructs that bear no relation to physiological bodily features, although they can function to stimulate or suppress them.

And *talismanic yantras* usually to promote planetary influences or to counteract unwanted planetary effects. These can be written on paper, on the skin of individuals or engraved on metals:
gold for the Sun and Jupiter
silver for the Moon
copper for Venus
brass for Mercury
and iron for Mars and Saturn.

Inks, like many ingredients of worship are prescribed in great detail, but would need to be locally sourced. Things like rose water added to the mix might be possible while many won't be, but as a basic minimum quill or fountain calligraphy pens show more dedication than ball point throw away pens.

For positive results lines are drawn from East to West; to defeat enemies they are drawn from West to East; for progress they are drawn upwards; to halt unwanted actions lines are drawn downwards.

For peace they should be created at midnight; for defence at noon; to attack enemies afternoon and evening, more serious cases at the latter; for other purposes the morning.

Sunday [Sun] is used for works of health, authority and affection, while chanting Oang Rang Raviaya Namah

Monday [Moon] love and attraction
with Oang Soong Somaya Namah

Tuesday [Mercury] for business
with Oang Hrang Hring Bung Buddhaya Namah

Wednesday [Jupiter] for good causes
with Oang Gung Gurvaya Namah

Thursday [Mars] litigation and dealing with enemies
with Ouang Bhaung Bhoumaya Namah

Friday [Venus] for love affairs
with Oang Sung Sukraya Namaha

Saturday [Saturn] for conflict
with Oang Eang Haring Sring Sani Charya Namaha

Magic squares for planets are also classed as yantras of the talismanic variety.

The *transcendental 3D zonule yantras* that make up the Mahashaktis as passed on from Dadaji all have planetary correspondences too and could be seen as like the Sephiroth Temples of the Quabalistic Tree to Westerners. We visualise ourselves inside these zonules with the elements that make up the yantra at respective levels between the bindu point above and 'four gates' motif around the base.
Some Goddesses share the same yantras, or variations on a theme of them , but each has her own unique mantra:
 Santoshi Ma and Ambika have similar yantras
Aghori and Kali share the same yantra
 Tripura and Lalita share the same yantra.

There are too numerous a number of yantras dedicated to deities or specific purposes to list them here but some of the major ones are for Ganesh, Parvati, Saraswati, Mahamritaji [Siva], Vishnu, Hanuman, Bangla Mukti, Bhairon, many Goddesses, the Yantra of Liberation, and Conqueror of Obstacles.

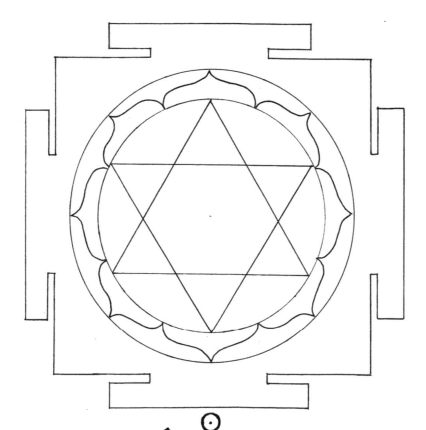

Santoshima

Young mother of Contentment

MANTRA:

Hreem Shri Santoshi Ma Mahamaye
Gaganandam Dayini
Shukravar Priye Devi
Narayani Namostute
Swaha!

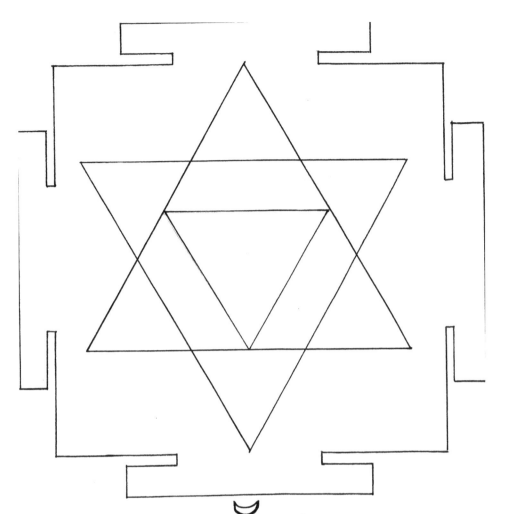

Shanti Devi
She of Peace & Union
Mantra:
Hreem sahana bhavatu sahanau blumaktu
Sahaviryam kavavā hai tejasi nāvadita mastu
Ma Vidvisārahi

Hrim sānti shānti shāntih
Swaha !

Tripura
She of abundance
Mantra:
Hreem Shareeng Hareeng Kaleeng
Shri Mahatripuraiya
Swaha!

Aghori
She of the cremation ground – not fearful
Mantra :
Hrim yam ram lam vam
Aghoraya ghortaraya namah
Swaha!

Digambari
Sky clad Devi
Mantra:

Hreem Digambara Digambara Shri Pada Villabh
Digambara
Swaha!

Kali
She of erotic magick of the Crone
Mantra:
Hreem Karing Kalikaya
Namah Swaha!

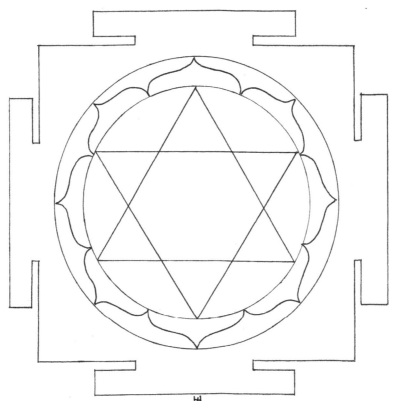

Ambika (Kausiki)
Mother of households & family
aspect of Parvati.

Mantra:
Hreem Kleem
Ambhoja Namah
Swaha!

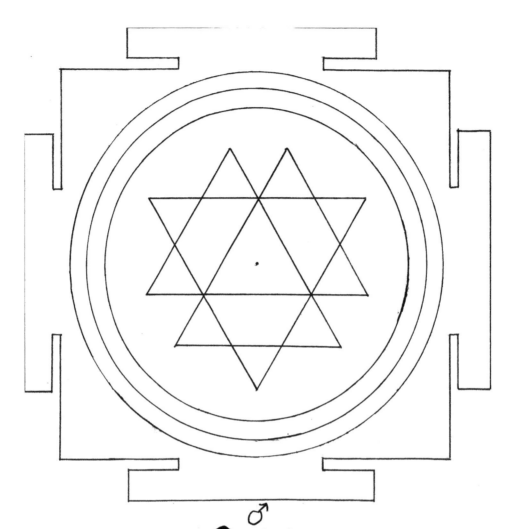

♂

DURGA
She of deliverence & Protection
Mantra:

Hreem Dum Durgayei Namaha
Swaha!

Alternative
Pentagram Yantra

Lalita

She offers perfect harmony & Union

Mantra:
Ka E I La Hreem
Ha Sa Ka La Hreem
Sa Ka La Hreem
Swaha!

The Evasive Kundulini

Dadaji stated in one of his essays that Kundulini Yoga and Laya Yoga were relatively recent inventions that had never led anyone to experience the Primary Clear Light, and that the coiled snake at the base of the spine, that could be raised by pranayama was only a symbol of the bodily alchemy that takes place when bodily shakti energy is aroused and unites with Siva consciousness.

It is known that Goraksnath used the meditation with his students, and also invented hatha yoga as a keep fit regime for the monastic system that he began in the 11th to 12th Centuries C.E. Kulavadhut, who has Vajrayana as well as Nath and Uttarakaula initiations, maintains that the meditation was originated by Nagajuna, a Buddhist reformer from around 150 to 250 C.E. However there are references to kundulini and hatha yoga in the later Upanishads, which are Vedic, rather than native Tamil texts gathered from 700 B.C.E. to the beginnings of the Common Era. 'The Krishna Yagurveda Upanishad' includes another minor Upanishad, the 'Yoga-Kundulini Upanishad.' They, like the Shakta Upanishads generally, are amongst the later texts, that fed into the emergence of the Indian Tantras of the 8th and 9th centuries along with native Tamil sources. Matseyendranath, Goraksnath's guru, in his 'Kaulajnana-Nirnaya,' dated to the 11th century speaks of the chakras, but makes no mention of kundulini.

Patanjali's 'Yoga Sutras' date from 400 C.E. and deal with yoga philosophy in a series of aphorisms. No mention is made of kundulini. He was a Tamil Shaivite. Yoga means *union* and we should not always assume that reference to it means hatha yoga.

So what do we make of all these dates? The Upanishads like much of Indian history are very difficult to date. Much depended on oral transmission, or even if texts were composed in one go they were copied, added to, and open to interpretation. In a large sub-continent like India, before the printing press there was no standardization. So it would seem that the 'Yoga-Kundulini Upanishad' is a later addition to the 'Krishna Yagurveda Upanishad,' using later concepts built up around a widespread symbol used in meditation, which itself had been used to represent bodily shakti and its union with Siva consciousness. It is certain that shakti energy dwells at the base on the spine and is associated with sexual energy, which in yab-yum can be reversed and turned inwards between partners. The chakras, although only tiny and cell like, do operate through the endrocrine glands. And pranayama: control of the breath, is the engine that excites the shakti energy. The two main nadis, Ida and Pingala do function through the nostrils. Breath is through the nostrils in cycles alternating from one to the other, with overlaps as these changes take over. This leads to the rod of Hermes glyph, known since Ancient Egypt and Babylon at least, that shows the two energies energising the lungs and internal organs in cyclic fashion. Their crossover points on the spine are the 'knots' that have to be cleared for free flow of energy. And coincide with the chakra centres. That much is all bodily physiology. Lotuses are the poetic creation of Hindu iconographers, and like our friend the snake will not be found in the body unless created there by visualisation.

In my experience, when bodily shakti, Kaulini Devi, was activated to unite with Siva consciousness the holistic experience transformed every cell of the physical and energy bodies, and no snake was involved. Slippery creatures snakes!

The Rise of Shakti Energy to Union with the Kaula Goddess

Om Gan Ganapati: Mulhadara of the Earth
The elephant of the Earth is with his cthonic rat.

Svadisthana of Water: the Dragon of the deep stirs his/her raw energy.

Manipura of Fire: the Ram of Spring does battle for his mate.

Anahata of Air: the gazelle has tamed Pashupatinath. The Higher Self is in play. Om Namah Sivaya.

Vishudda of Aether: the elephant returns as a God: Om Gan Ganapati namah.

Ajna of the third eye: is single, like Odin's: one pointed focus.

Sahasrara: Siva does not count petals on a lotus as his gaze is fused into the Clear Light Energy of Lalita.

Hreem Shreem Kleem Aim Sauh Lalita swaha!

Carl Jung on 'Kundulini' Yoga.

Esoteric East-West crossover groups are certain to be involved in syncretic studies of cross- cultural spiritual practices, by definition. A great pioneer in comparative sources for psychological analysis was Sigmund Freud's one-time Swiss pupil Carl Gustav Jung 1875-1961. Beyond Freud's pioneering but narrow patriarchal ideas on the symbols of the unconscious mind, by extending his studies into symbols Jung found in Hermetic Philosophy, Quabalism, Alchemy and its Egyptian origins [Khem an old name for Egypt], Eastern Philosophy, Native American and African sources he achieved a synthesis which revealed a deeper level to the mind than just the personal subconscious Freud identified, but also a common level of what he named the Collective Unconscious where dialects of common symbols existed and had a formative background effect in shaping consciousness from the deep mind. These he called Archetypes of the Collective Unconscious. I have studied Jung's ideas from when I was a student 40-50 years ago but was only made aware recently of the collection of four lectures from 1932 that were gathered together with numerous appendices to form a book, in the Bollingen series, that was later called 'The Psychology of Kundulini Yoga'

These were early days for Westerners to be studying Eastern ideas. Jung had previously written on the Indian 'Rig Veda', 'Upanishads', and 'Yoga Sutras' of Patanjali, and collaborated with Richard Wilhelm on the Chinese Taoist Oracle, the 'I Ching', and on the Buddhist meditations of the 'Secret of the Golden Flower'. In the early 1960s the only popularly available books on yoga dealt only with hatha yoga as a system of keep fit exercises, with maybe a page that touched on meditation as an add-on. To look more deeply into the psychology behind yoga Jung and a group of associates had to turn to the translations and commentaries of Sir John Woodroffe [aka Arthur Avalon], usually of Tantrik texts, done whilst he was a High Court judge in the British Raj occupation of India. That was an era of Victorian morality based on supposedly Christian values but in reality far more repressive social engineering. So his writings were often shortened, censored or bowdlerised. Natives suspicious of cultural theft as well as the exploitation of natural resources did not always divulge reliable information and often employed sandhaya bhasa, the twilight, secret, language to encode the meanings in their texts. I have two translations of the 'Kulanava Tantra', one by Woodroffe and one by a native translator. The former is in an easier style for an English speaker to follow but the latter is far longer and reveals that Woodroffe missed sections and whole chapters out.

The text chosen by Jung and associates to focus on was taken from 'The Serpent Power': a relatively ancient but not especially Tantrik piece called 'Sat-Chakra-Niripana'. Jung gives this a **PSYCHOLOGICAL** commentary, which focusses on the symbolism given for the chakras. I emphasize 'psychological' as there is no attempt to discus practical yogic activity in any way, even though he mentions an Indian native who emphasised to him that the chakras are a physical reality and not just mental concepts. Endocrinology, the study of the functioning of the endocrine glands in secreting hormones into the body was still relatively in its infancy, having slowly grown, over 70 or so years before Jung's lecture, from isolated experiments, while the centres had been discovered by yogic introspection many centuries before. The symbols that evolved to represent the chakras owe more to the ingenuity of Indian illustrators to depict descriptions of yogis observations than anything that could be found in nature. Yet it was these that Jung made the centre of discussion. He did not mention the main 'nadis' ida, pingala, and sushuma except in passing, as they relate to controlled breathing as a practical activity that is the engine to stimulate shakti energy, symbolised as a sleeping snake at the base of the spine. Also, somewhat naïve by the publishers was the use of the Sri Yantra on the cover of the collection of lectures, as this only has oblique connections to the chakras via the alternate male and female triangles at the centre of the yantra. Little is made of the Goddess's role of shakti energy, which is central to Sri Vidya, and certainly no mention of the spellcraft of related magic sigils. A figure in full lotus asana, familiar from many texts on yoga, and with chakra 'lotuses' in place up the spine does accompany the Sat-Chakra-Nirpana inside the book and that would have made a more appropriate cover.

Jung's great service in his synthesis of worldwide archetypes threw up one central symbol that his symbology rested on: that of the mandala, a term he adopted from Tibetan Buddhist and Bon multi-symmetrical circular icons for meditation, which he found dialectic variants of around the globe, in such diverse forms as cathedral stained glasses, to magic circles of Eurasian 'shamen', their remnants in witchcraft, elaboration in quabalistic magic, even in Native American practices, where emigrating tribes had taken then when crossing Bering Straits ice bridges. All had a variant of the equal arm cross within the circle, which Jung identified with the five elements of mental function: earth with sensation, water with intuition, fire with emotion, air with intellect, and aether at the centre point above for abstract thought. When we reach the 'Sat-Chakra-Niripana', Jung basically sequences these elements in ascending order as he discusses the chakras. He uses the chakra names as taken from the accompanying diagram:

Muladhara: the base chakra of the scrotum, he naturally

identifies with **Earth**, and roots, where he alludes to an Indian woman who kept dreaming of being entangled in roots, which after studying Woodroffe he interpreted as her earthly duties and and social interactions preventing her from what she thought should be her spiritual unfoldment. In bodily terms he associated the chakra with **instincts** like childbirth and defecation. The symbol within the chakra of an elephant was easily understood as the solidity of the physical world. Ganesh, Siva's elephant headed son is accompanied by a rat, symbolising his cthonic power in relation to the underworld.

Svadhisthana, of the place of 'gut reactions' : borrowing Sanskrit terms and cautious language of the time is applied by Jung to the sex organs, and the **Water** element, and hence, we are left to deduce, to sexual fluids, and urine. This is, again obliquely, referred to as the emergence of Shakti energy and linked to the word 'kundulini'. But that is about the only mention of the word as he instead refers to the large fish that is the chakra's symbol and refers to it as a Leviathan symbol

"here be dragons" as it says in old maps of the sea for unknown monsters of the deep in the Water element. We are left, nowadays, to make the link between the symbol and sexual activity. As we can also say now: Shakti energy is aroused by ecstatic sexual and ritual yogic activity. Presently we could also expand on woman's monthly cycle, its movement around the nadis and how shakti energy can be stimulated in the nadis with acupressure and skilful foreplay.

As shakti energy rises we reach the solar plexus centre of the **Manipura** chakra, which Jung equates with **Fire** and emotion. This centre is activated when soldiers go into battle or we experience conflict situations, but here is harnessed to upward movement. The chakra symbol here is the ram,: Aries, a creature who peaks in Spring for contests with other males as part of courtship rituals leading to coupling with females.

The heart chakra, **Anahata** Jung associates with **Air**, where [in the term he coined] 'individuation' begins as the shakti energy is brought into balance when instinctual urges are diminished, mental activity is clearer, but ego also emerges. Quabalists might want to equate this to the Knowledge and Conversation of the Guardian Spirit as selfish motives then begin to fall away. The symbol that goes with the chakra is the gazelle, a fairly mild natured creature by now [I thought of Siva Pasupatinath, Lord of the Animals too, as wild nature is tamed.]

The **Visuddha** chakra is at the **Aether** level where mantra gives form to force [the Vision and the Voice of Enochian Aethers.] The elephant appears again here as symbol of the chakra, but not the solid variety of earthly muladhara, but where Gods, Goddesses and spirits take visionary form: Ganesh as God, not lord of the world and underworld.

The **Ajna** chakra is the third eye, organ of light, of the brow: the pituitary gland that secretes the honey elixir of Sauh. The chakra symbol is a two-petalled lotus, which resembles an eye. The eye is single, like Odin's: only focussed now on inner consciousness.

Of the **Sahasrara** chakra of the crown Jung says nothing can be said. It has no qualities. The 'thousand petalled lotus' of chakra symbolism is not a place where petals can be counted. It is the place of total Siva consciousness absorbed in the primary clear light of Shakti energy.

It has to be said that the chakra sequence that Woodroffe and Jung used is not the only one, but one of competing descriptions. This is because the endocrine glands do not perfectly match the chakras as stated above, but the introspection that discovered them sometimes combined the functions of neighbouring glands in what it identified was the chakras: the thymus gland is in the same region as the heart and contributes to the function of that 'chakra'; little mentioned by endocrinologists are the lyden glands that contribute to functions of the Svadhisthana in sex hormone production, and the pineal as well as the pituitary are both in the sphere of the head, and both contribute to the Ajna 'chakra's' function. Each chakra has been given a mandala by Indian icon painters.

It has also to be said that using the Umbra Zonule cone of meditation, when the cone is viewed from the bindu point that represents the Sahasrara, looking down, each mandala would fit inside the one below it to create a grand mandala.

Jung does make the observation that Indians have a culture where these higher levels of consciousness are taken for granted, while in the West we are usually struggling with the psychology of the lower levels of consciousness, and that is the usual domain of clinical psychology. Sadly Jung's depth psychology has been overtaken in general clinical practice by more functionalist approaches of cognitive and behavioural psychologies used to fit people into everyday social patterns [which we called 'rat psychology' when students].

Quabalists would recognise a parallel in Middle Pillar Otz Chiim exercises of Rising up the Planes; Malkuth for Muladhara, through Universe trump XXI to Yesod/ Svadhisthana, through the Art trump to Tiphereth/Anahata, through the Priestess trump to Kether/ Sahasrara. In fact that was the ritual I used while assuming a dialect of Siva's Godform as Pan/Pasupatinath before being fully acquainted with Tantrik techniques, but I do thank the Priestess for her part in crossing the Abyss. Fruition is not the gradual process of the celibate yogi, which can take more than one incarnation to complete it is said, but the Thunderbolt that illuminates all in one holistic flash.......then you have to figure out the grindingly slow process of grounding, and how to bring siddhis back under control to be able to continue with everyday life: rebirth after transformation.

A Daily Practice Regime

Newcomers to Tantrik yoga, and those who have asked to take initiation often ask about a daily routine that they can adopt. This is essential in a way that once per week visits to a church are useless, as it is not buildings or even a community but the self which are key to personal inner development:

In the science of consciousness the laboratory is body and mind.

Preparation

The key elements of practice here are relaxation, deep even breathing [pranayama], concentration and visualisation to give form to abstract archetypal energies we call deities, and meditative detachment from everyday thought. Raja yoga uses the force of will to enforce this vacuous state, but it is not the only way to deal with the endless flow of mental activity, and certainly not a means suitable to many people. A more Taoist approach is to see this endless flow of thought as a stream passing by, and not to be drawn into its flow, but remaining a detached observer. So when directing the imagination to formulate images and concentrate on mantras this mental flow only becomes a background that does not get involved with our central focussed concentrations.

If visualisation does not come easily to you paint a geometric shape, like a triangle or circle, and fill it in with a bright primary colour [red or green are most effective] on a white card background. Or cut the shape from a plain sheet of coloured paper and paste it to a plain white sheet of card. When seated comfortably place the card image directly in your line of sight. Relax, breath deeply and evenly and stare at the shape for a minute, then close your eyes so that the after-image, which is the diametric opposite in colour to your shape on the card, will appear. See how long you can hold this inner image for. Do this as often as you can, but at least daily, until you feel you are getting good at it. When you come to build more complex inner images don't expect them to to be as clear cut, with the detail of a T.V. or computer screen image, but expect images more like those on the edges of the dream state.

There is nothing fixed and formalised about what follows. It evolved out of practice and can evolve further to suit individual temperaments and progress. It takes me about 45 minutes every morning, but for those still working for an employer that is unlikely to be possible, so the evening will probably be preferred. The framework of the practice is for use by one person, but the same framework can be applied for a couple to practice, and in the more elaborate practices mentioned in the *Uttarakaula initiations* script found elsewhere in the section above about initiations. It is written from a male viewpoint initially, but I will also point to how to polarize things for female practitioners.

Get to know your work space as being within a mandala of the four directions. Face East, visualised bright yellow/white; South will be to your right, red; West blue, behind you; and North, dark green, to your left. You can put prints or small sculptures in the quarters to aid visualisations. You only need worry about taking a hatha yoga pose if you are already practised in this work. A comfortable chair facing East [it may be other directions for activities other than this daily practice] in which you can keep your spine erect, with or without cushion adjustments, will achieve the same ends. Keep your feet free of footwear to aid grounding energies rather than insulating your body from the Earth. Deliberately think about any tension in your muscles and relax to let it go. Then begin deep breathing, as deep as you can at first: a count of 9 in, hold for 9, breathe out slowly for 9 and hold it in for 9 if you can manage it. Try that for 4 cycles to counter the short and shallow breath of everyday living. Then lower it to a cycle of 7s and strive to maintain it for the length of the practice.

Mantra Yoga and Visualisations

The Sanskrit mantras are used to fix the mind on the abstract energies in the form of deities evoked from your deep mind. Artistic portrayals may help at first, but Indian images tend to be richly detailed and ultimately they need to be your own formulations so are best seen as naked: forms that we all know. Their qualities may be helped by iconic portrayals showing symbolic weapons or other objects, but avoid symbolic multiple limbs as they do not make visualisation easy. Familiarise yourself with the symbols and demeanour of the deity until you get the feel of their presence. Consider yourself in the primal state of nakedness too. If you use incense whirl it 3 times around your working space. Its not essential for daily practice, but do keep a wholesome drink beside you [I use herb tea] to sprinkle the deities and anoint yours and their chakras as an offering. Waft the drink with incense if you are using it.

The OPENING [Sprinkle and visualise as you invoke]

First, face East and greet Ganesh, the elephant headed son of Siva and Parvati with
"Om Gam Ganapati please guide and protect us in our rites"
Then repeat the mantra to the other 3 quarters, remaining seated, but visualise, in the appropriate colours, for the individual quarters, with Him standing with a trident at each quarter.

" **Om Shiva-Shakti** " to the East. Visualise them beneath Mount Kailash, then moving to your shrine.
Below and left: **"Hreem Kreem Kali** please guide and protect the animals and the planet"

centre" **Hreem Kleem Lalita Tripura"** please guard the children
and right **"Hreem Kleem Lalita"**
[the Triple Goddess in her old, middle-aged and youthful aspects]

behind, to the left of the quarter, **"Om Siva Pasupatinath"** [Lord of animals/Pan aspect]
behind to the right of the quarter, " **Hrim Dum Durgayai,** please guide and protect the family of Kaulas great mother."
mark their images [photos or visualised] with the liquid to draw triangles, apex up for Siva or pointing downwards for aspects of the Goddess.

INVOCATION OF SIVA to the point centrally above your mandala to create a cone of power:

"Om Namah Shivaya". Sprinkle his image, the quarters and above

"Sivohim" [if male: "I am Siva"] touch your chakras in turn with juice. Or your partner or image of Siva if female**"Om Siva Pashupatinath of the forests and the fields.
Om Siva Shakti"**

INVOCATION OF SHAKTI to join Siva at the apex of the mandala cone:

Hreem Kleem Lalita
They embrace facing South. Lalita swirls her sari off and around the mandala to fill the star-spangled cone of maya, embraces Siva from the right, then behind and then left, moving around him,

unfurls her hair, and spirals down the cone of power to the mandala to join with Pashupatinath. Depending if the practitioner is male or female, so will they embrace on the meditation chair, as if in it, or facing the partner. In full rituals with this can often be a real couple and a reclining position is more useful for foreplay.

Siva invokes the Triple Goddess in his partner [image or visualisation]:

Hreem Kreem Kali; Hreem Kleem Lalita; Hreem Kleem Lalita Tripura.

Energy is cycled from the female/Goddess crown chakra to basal, up though male/Siva basal to crown in reverse current to male 'missionary style' sex activity. As ecstasy is achieved through female orgasm, real or visualised, a shortened version of the Sri Vidya mantra is intoned

Hreem Shreem Kleem Aim Lalita Tripura Sauh at least 3 times, then

Hreem Shreem Kleem Aim Lalita Sauh, similarly at least 3 times.

Your tongue should be curled up under the pallet when intoning **Sauh** and the shakti nectar will shower participants from crown chakras downward.

Remain in united formless meditation while concentration lasts.

Conclude with

Hreem Kleem Lalita; Om Siva Pahupatinath; Om Siva Shakti; Om Mane Padme Hum! As Siva and Shakti spiral back to Lake Manasarova [in the 'Himalayas'] for splashdown and return to Mount Kailash, and the Clear Light of Shakti energy.

Thank all other deities as they return to their realms. Ground yourself with the Taoist Arch or visualise energy returning to earth though the chakra in the bawls of the feet.

Om Mane Padme Hum

Notes on the mantras above:

Om: the supreme sound of the universe. Used to to begin male mantras.

Aim: the female equivalent of Om, used to start female mantras.

Ganapati: the phonetic sound used for Ganesh in mantra.

Om namah Shivaya: reverence [namah] for Siva.

Hreem: opens the heart chakra.

Kreem energizes.

Kleem is magnetic: draws forces in, as in invocation.

Shreem is lunar.

Lalita is the supreme goddess, the playful one. Lalita Tripura is her triple form, maiden, mature, and elderly, like Kali.

Dum: is the protective mantra of Durga

Om Mane Padme Hum: the jewel is in the lotus.

From **Sri Vijnana Bhairava Tantra**, amongst the oldest of all the tantras. [Chapter70]:

Said Siva:

"Oh Queen of the Gods, the bliss of woman is attained even in the absence of a consort. By fully remembering and absorbing the mind in the experience of kissing, hugging and foreplay the bliss swells for either partner if they practice alone."

Because of its close attachment to deep 'survival of species' instinct erotic fantasy is a strong means of developing visualisation skills.

Mantras to bring deities to in-dwell statues

For Siva: Om Am Hreem Kram Yam Ram Lam

Vam Saam Saam Saam Ham Ksam
Hamsah-Soham
Sivaji Jiva iha sthital.

For Devi: Am Hreem Krom Yam Ram Lam Vam
Saam Saam Saam Ham Ksam
Hamsah- Soham
Devyah Jiva iha sthitah

For Ganesh: Om Am Kriim Krom Yam Ram Lam Vam
Saam Saam Ham Ksam
Hamsa-Soham
Ganapati Jiva iha sthitah.

Repeat 7 times for yourself for each chakra, and once for the sculpture's chakra points anointing with incense and salt water mixed

Roadmaps for the Soul:
Art Therapy / A Visual Magic Cosmology.

Like Surrealism, Art that seeks to mine and record images from the depths of the deep mind has been employed by Art Therapists and psychic explorers to understand their own psycho-physical makeup and make it intelligible to others in many ways throughout history. Some have used such art as teaching aids to others wishing to follow similar paths of exploration. This can take the form of pre-determined iconography of a tradition which allows little scope for variation, such as Russian Orthodox religious icons or even Tibetan thankas, or more creative expressions of personal growth of psychic unfoldment as is found in Art Therapy or individual fetishes. I have seem the Art therapist referred to as being a modern Shaman, [Shaun McNiff 'Art as Medicine'], with a mode of operation that goes on, or takes another participant on, an inward journey of soul recovery, then using Art, either visual, written or encapsulated into music,dance and drama, to record the discoveries of that journey. That comparison seems to fit well. But you don't have to be a medicine man to be a psychic explorer. Such Art is for the individual for self discovery as well as recovery.

Crucial to all forms of art which has its origins in psychic exploration is the diary, sketchbook, or notebook to record the discoveries from the inner world. The best place to keep this document is beside your bed to write down dreams and *ground them* before the memories fly away. The analysis of their content can wait for daytime and the conscious mind. Its also useful to carry a notebook on your daytime travels too, to record daydreams, meditations, and reflections on the dreamtime symbolism. From this raw psychic energy you can then work up images to be employed in finished art forms.

In the 21st century we are fortunate to be liberated, if we wish to be, from the confines of religious dogma, and able to partake in creative paths of self enquiry, but we will still need some form of cosmology in which to frame our discoveries, and for me this came in the broadest and non-sectarian framework for interpretation that is to be found in the psychological analyses of Swiss psychologist Carl Jung [1875-1961] who sought to get behind the cultural veneers that overlay the common symbols of psychic unfoldment that lay behind them . These he called *archetypes*. His sources for research include the writing and diagrams of Alchemists from Egypt [the science of Khem, an old name for Egypt] like Zozimos, to Paracelsus; Quabalists and Hermetic Philosophers like Agrippa; Chinese Taoism, and the I Ching; Oriental and 'primitive' religious manifestations generally; and Western religious imagery, in a non-sectarian way, as a complete cultural overview of religious and philosophical thinking and its associated artistic manifestations.

Archetype is only one word that has passed into common usage thanks to Jung, who actually coined several terms now used in psychological jargon: another example being *'persona'*, which means the external image of ourselves that we present to the world, or others see us as. Jung extended Freud's idea of the unconscious to include not only the personal pool of remnants of personal experience that make up dreams in encoded forms, but placed that pool on the edge of the oceanic *Collective Unconscious*, where the archetypes exist, and have an ordering function around which personal psychic material gathers to create personalised symbolism. These, he concluded, could be recovered from the unconscious by initiatory rites of passage or analytic psychology leading to *Individuation* as he named it, establishing growth towards self discovery and Enlightenment. The archetypes, he decided, were formed through evolution by the persistent effects of primitive experience. Genetics and Austin Spare's *Atavistic Resurgence* seem to confirm this assertion.

The main archetypes Jung identified were:
the *Earth Mother;*
Divine Child [Krishna, Horus, Jesus etc.];
the *Sun; Moon; Sky;*

Anima [man's idea of woman] and *Animus* [woman's idea of man], giving rise to Gods and Goddesses;

the *Shadow* [all that we don't like about ourselves driven into the unconscious, from where it must be recovered in order to regain psychic wholeness;

the *Daemon,* or higher self, that guides the individual through initiation, or individuation in Jungian terminology; and

the *Wise Old Man or Magna Mater* [the life guide or Guru who teaches from practical experience.]

All of these can be identified as stages of psychic unfoldment once cultural veneers have been peeled away. For instance the Wise Old Man might appear as a ship's captain as a symbol of a guide for a journey, [that is life.] The word archetype has at times been given broader meaning to include terms like 'hero archetype', and so it is possible to regard all of the Tarot trumps as archetypes. Indeed there is a Jungian tarot set designed by Robert Wang, although I don't agree with all his attributions. The very multiplicity of tarot decks displays how archetypal patterns can appear in a variety of individual dialects.

Thanks to Sting and Police [the Rock group] the word *synchronicity* has passed in to more common usage. Jung coined it to mean a meaningful coincidence with no obvious causal connecting principle, suggestive of forces not explainable by, and therefore appealing to known science. Oracles like the Taoist I Ching, or tarot cards seem to be operated by such forces and pre-suppose spiritual rather than just materialistic dimensions to the multiverse. Salvador Dali's *Paranoic Critical Activity,* where multiple layers of imagery overlay each other, mimic such a universe. Herman Rorschach's ink blot test, where psychiatric patients are asked what images they see in random shapes, and thus reveal their own inner mental workings in a similar way. These projected internal images can be worked up into art which is unique to each person's perceptions, although related to the same stimulus if more than one person uses it as a starting point.

Recourse to other source material of the material world may be needed to transform the psychic material into recognisable art, rather than using only imagination to create objets d' art. Automatic drawing and writing like that of Austin Spare or other Surrealists, or the cut up poetry that William Burroughs and others employed also works in this way, once meaning is attached to it.

After the stage of initiation or individuation reintegrating the disliked personal personality traits that have built the *shadow* archetype Jung identified the *mandala* archetype, which can appear in Art, or even in dreams as symbols like the crossroads. He found examples of this not only in the oriental meditation icons which he took the name from, but in such culturally diverse places as circular stained glass windows and the magician's working space of the magic circle. The archetype is that of balance and is typically built around the equal armed cross of the four elements balanced at the centre as the quintessence, and is often sub-divided into eight sectors on which figurative or abstract patterning is repeated. Jung also associated the four main psychic activities with these elements:

intuition

thinking feeling

sensation

which are also brought back into balance, where previously people tend to function in dominant and less in subordinate areas. This state of restored psychic balance Jung experienced himself after the turmoil that accompanied his break with Freud and his limited observations that had taken on the form of a patriarchal dogma. Not only did he find himself building mandala shape constructions in his garden, but like many in the same state of recovery, experienced visions and dreams of wholeness as life's initiation process became complete.

Mystics have a variety of models of the universe, such as the quabalistic tree, and a relation to them by which to judge progress, but to me Jung's model seems to have been gleaned from the most far reaching and cross cultural sources. So if you are a psychonaut or are encouraging others in self discovery, keep a lookout for the archetypes we have mentioned, in yours and others art, drama, music or dreams, and if you see through the camouflaged symbolism through which they are appearing they can prove useful signposts on your inner journey. Spontaneous creations are always the most fruitful ones, rather than those created by being led, but if the signs appear be ready to read to read them.

Uttarakaula Lineage

There has been much dis-information posted on the Internet about the Uttarakaula tradition line that descended from Pagalababa of Ranchi, which has been copied into books and sites, so it seems necessary to set records straight:

Shri Dadaji Gurudev Mahendranath [1911-1991] became the first European to receive Indian Sannyasi initiation, when he arrived in India in 1953, from Shri Lokanath Maharaj into the Adi Nath Sampradaya, who claim descent from Matseyendranath. Further travels to Bihar and Bengal led to initiation into the Uttarakaula Tantrik Tradition by Pagalababa of Ranchi. At a time when communications were less well developed than in the 21st century Dadaji thought that Pagalababa was the last guru of that tradition, and when he died he thought the lineage would become extinct in India, as would the Adi Nath line, although the Nath Acara is a vast network of sub sects based on the teachings of Goraksnath, a pupil of Matseyendranath. Goraksnath's ideas were designed for the development of monastic disciplines, unlike his those of his teacher. So Dadaji had made plans for international groups to carry the lines forward because of the effects of Westernisation on the Indian population. He did initiate a native Indian into Adi Nath line: now Yogiraj Gurunath Siddhanath, as well as Westerners, to spread the Nath principles worldwide. What he did not know because of poor communications in India was that Thakar Kalachand, who had received initiation in the Uttara line from Pagal Haranath had not only initiated Pagalababa but also a female guru, Maheshwari Ma, who in turn, had initiated Kulavadhut of Sikkim, and who is still alive and well in 2015. Therefore the native Indian lineage did not die with Mahendranath, but instead thrives, alongside the international group that Dadaji began. Any decision on Dadaji's part to fuse Adi Nath and Uttarakaula traditions was not therefore within the scope of decision making available to him, and neither of the native lines did become extinct with his death.

It seems highly likely that there are other branches of the Uttara tree that Dadaji was unaware of too, as is seen in the two branches created by Thakar Kalachand in Pagalababa and Maheshwari Ma, that reveal that in the tradition there is not necessarily a history of having to have an absolute solitary guru figure.

```
                    Pagal Haranath
                          I
                   Thakar Kalachand
                          I
       Pagalababa----------------------------Maheshwari Ma
            I                                     I
       Mahendranath                          Kulavadhut
```

Pagalababa

Kula Avadhut

Was initiated into Uttarakaula by Aghori Baba and Maheshwari Ma when he was five years old in the cremation ground of Vakreshwar, West Bengal, which is one of 51 Tantrik vortexes of India.

He did 29 years study of Buddhist Tantra and Christian Gnosticism.

Aged 12 Ram Nath Aghori Baba empowered him with the final practice of the Aghori School.

Aged 18 he had further Tantrik initiations at Turapnath, West Bengal.

He studied Vedanta with Baba Thakar and Maha Mudra of Tilopa Order and was named Satpurananda Avadhut, aged 19.

He studied at Kolkata Universary.

He was also initiated into Mastang, the wrathful Sufi tradition, by Mastang Darbash Shah of the Bangladeshi Master line.

He took Sannyasi Diksha in 1984 with Anandamayee Ma.

He was given the Baul Chinnamani title in 1993.

He was Best Scholar of Tantrik Buddhism at the Research Institute of Tibet in Gangtok, Sikkim in 1994, and received 4 other academic awards.

His final Sahaja Nath initiation in the tradition of Bangladesh was from Brahmamayee Ma in 1995.

He was named Tantra King at Kamakaya Pith, Assam in 2004.

He is regarded as a Siddha in the Tibetan and Sikkimese Buddhist Tradition and expounds the Blue Way of Tara Kula Krama.

Kulavadhut

Maheshwari Ma

Reincarnation.

Enlightened beings like the Dalai Lama and other Tolkus [known Tibetan reincarnations] probably come to mind when the word reincarnation is used. Other traditions like Hinduism have provided examples, like Sai Baba quite recently, who was worshipped for his most recent incarnation, but equally for the life before, which he remembered vividly in his childhood, and of course there are numerous examples in India if anyone cares to look. Belief in Transmigration of Souls was pretty much worldwide before the patriarchal theologians decided to stamp out the traditional beliefs and associated practices to replace them with notions of everlasting heaven and hell which provided a better means of psychological coercion for social control. Emperor Justinian [483-565 C.E.] at the time of the early Byzantine Christian Church, for one, had all that he thought were references to it in their bible removed. Emperors can do that.

The Tulkus and others like them are of course specialised cases who have worked to gain knowledge of states of consciousness that relate to those associated with the after death realms known as Bardos by Tibetans, since the era of the Bon religion was established. But three decades ago when the English T.V. Channel 4 was in its infancy and vowed to screen a less predictable menu of programmes than the established channels, it presented a two hour documentary about six ordinary Australians who had undergone regressive hypnosis with a psychologist to recover memories of past lives. Their utterances were recorded, and passports checked to see that they had not been out of Australia before they were taken to the locations they had identified, so as to rule out any prior knowledge that could have been gained during their present life.

I remember three of the six cases explored on the programme. One man recalled life that included living on the gun deck of a sailing ship in the navy of Admiral Horatio Nelson, famous for his part in the battle of Trafalgar [1805 C.E.] against Napoleon

Bonaparte's French Navy. The man recalled manning the cannon and the harsh regime that sailors were subjected to below decks, by whippings meted out by the officer in charge of the deck. He recalled his dying moments as a cannonball smashed through the timbers of the ship and he succumbed to severe injury. The voice the hypnotised subject was speaking in was deeper and gruffer than his waking voice and in a dialect that matched the time and place of the former life when checked. Naval records also confirmed the existence of the ship, the man, and officers' names revealed under hypnosis.

The programme's stunning progression of cases that caused me to remember them next involved a young lady, who had been killed, also when she was a young woman, who had been working in a library in Dresden, in Germany when the city was subjected to a severe aerial bombardment near the end of World War Two. The case was interesting that the life had been cut short and that she had been reborn quite quickly in terms of Earth years, it is possible to conjecture, because her destiny had not been fulfilled. Remarkably, the library had been one of the few buildings in the town to have survived the bombing, and the young woman, in the new life had been able to reveal to the researchers, what books were on which shelves [still], even the contents of obscure and rarely read volumes in a different language to her Australian English, covered in dust, when researchers went to check the story. When narrow-minded 'scientists' try to explain away such sources of information to suit their own version of reality they always manage to come up with ideas that are far more bizarre than what is staring them in the face, to account for how it had come about.

Equally extraordinary was the case of the woman who had been alive in England during the Dissolution of the Monasteries after the split from Roman Catholicism by Henry VIII [reigned 1507–47]. Her husband in that life had used slabs of masonry from Glastonbury Abbey, to build a cottage for them to live in. That was something she had found sacrilegious, as she held prevailing

Christian values of the time and she seems to have led a pious life as a result. While in Australia and under hypnosis she had drawn a spiral shape and said that it was on the floor of the cottage. When the team of investigators arrived in Glastonbury, 400 years after these events, even the course of the nearby river had changed, but at length she orientated herself to the landscape and managed to find the cottage, which had survived because of its solid stone construction, and as farmers had used it as a cow shed. When they spoke to the then, incredulous, owner and asked if they could investigate the structure, he agreed. After shovelling away the layers of cow dung they did indeed find a Celtic spiral on the floor which the lady had drawn halfway across the world! Long distance cow dung scientists will no doubt have a suitable explanation as to how this could have occurred.

Although six studies could almost be called anecdotal, the psychologist had a very large study group which was not part of the presentation. From those that were presented I would like to point to a couple of observations: one that I already mentioned before, that it seemed that where a life was cut off prematurely the soul entity seems to rejoin the life stream quickly in terms of Earth years in order to fulfil the karmic attractions that caused them to incarnate before. Conversely 'well lived' lives[however that could be defined] could lead to time away from the planet of hundreds of Earth years existing in the inter-life bardos. That is suggested in the' Bardo Thodol', or 'Book of the Dead', of Tibet in the Sidpa bardo, of becoming: that doesn't always mean becoming human again, but various realms according to the level of the entity's development, or the animal realms or those of hungry ghosts, away from the Earth. Another observation is that people investigated were all born back into the same sex.

We all know of lives that have ended in extreme emotional trauma that have caused the soul entities to become Earthbound until released by effective exorcism to move the entity on to beneficial realms not just away from the person or thing being haunted. I used to live near a church with a church exorcist, and the whole damn village was full of wandering spirits he'd released to just wander! Life is only a projection from the Absolute state and many souls are not going to have moved into higher consciousness [of the Chikhai bardo] so their psychological make-up will likely lead into some very uncomfortable places if they are not given the guidance through the intermediate state of the Chonyid bardo and the bardo of becoming: traditionally 49 earth days before physical rebirth or birth into other realms. It is likely to be far longer for all bar Tolkus.

I was lucky enough to find a psychic who I trusted not to be a deluded fraud and who helped me to recover more memories of past lives than those I had remembered parts of, and which she expanded upon. Means of death is a common memory and can create aversions in present lives, like aversion to water if you drowned. I remembered that, and having been stabbed. Bringing those memories into consciousness has the effect of clearing a subconscious knot so dream diaries are important. Seeing all the lives joined up like a jigsaw stretching into way back beyond sent a shiver of shakti energy up my spine! Mitzi, the psychic could provide data that was checkable against Earth records, so lifted her further in my estimation of how genuine she was. The visions seen in inter-life bardos vary according to individual psychology, experiences while living, and patterns of indoctrination.

The After Death Bardos.

In 'Nu Tantras' I started the process of trying to create a secular version of the Bardo Thodol, Tibetan Book of the Dead, for those not brought up as Buddhists, and using more general archetypes than the deities that that school of Buddhism would relate to. The Bardo Thodol is intended to be read to the deceased as a guide to what they will experience in the post mortem state. Not all of us are going to have someone willing to spend over a month doing such readings for us, and most won't know anyone who has even heard of the texts. Neither can we predict accidents or events that take place far away from home. So it strikes me that anyone who does have an interest in the post-mortem bardos would be well advised to make themselves aware of the territory we will all enter when we die, to become master/mistress of our own destiny.

Bon and Buddhist masters who have memories of inter-life mental/spiritual states have made very similar texts on the subject, and there is ample evidence from Bon Tantras that the Tibetan Buddhist version is built on the older tradition, but with some doctrinal tweaking about deities. So new dialects are always in a state of evolution to create psychological slants that support religious viewpoints. And what you put in on Earth is what you will experience beyond. The abstract levels that support the imagery demonstrate a consistency. There are 6 bardos: 3 on Earth and 3 after/ between. We don't need to concern ourselves with the earthly bardos here.

Time scale is also only symbolic: 49 'days' in the bardos, but souls can stay in the bardos for hundreds of years and Earth time is irrelevant. It is said that it is three and a half days after heart and breath have ceased when we realise we are dead, and that memory is many times stronger, even if we are emerging from terminal senility.

Signs of Approaching Death. [Doctrine of the Six Lights]

Bon and Buddhist traditions agree on this, based on the collapse of the 'elements' that have built the body:

Earth into water as the body loses weight

Water into fire as urine, blood, sex fluids and phlegm dry up

Fire into air as breathing becomes difficult and the body loses heat: by head [bad karma] or

feet [good karma], go cold.

Air into aether as the tongue turns blue, the sense of touch is lost, and space like, Clear White Light envelops consciousness.

CHIKHAI BARDO

With the appearance of the Clear Light [as Siva consciousness is aware of and united with the primeval Shakti energy, if you happen to be Shaivite or Shakta...... or otherwise hold other doctrinal notions to explain this experience] in Tibetan terms you have entered the first post-mortem state they call the Chikhai Bardo. For those seeking Liberation from rebirth this is the desired end and you can seek to maintain that state.

CHONYID BARDO

Once visions start to appear out of the Light you are potentially on the road to re-incarnation, drawn back by karmic connections to the Earth. But Liberation is still possible on the bardo planes. The visions will be of your own making based on Earthly experience and indoctrination you have received.

As you proceed through visionary experiences watch and listen, but don't attach feelings to what you experience, or hope to go back to where you were on Earth. Their form is moulded by karma and past experience on Earth. Remain detached. If you are tempted to engage with them think of your favourite deity or spiritual teacher [it could just as easily be Jesus or one of the Marys, even though they were not Tibetan, we are dealing with abstract principles not doctrines.]

In Tibetan, and most other traditions at some point we find the multi symmetrical patterns of balance called mandalas, whether they be the magic circle or cathedral stained glass windows, or the Asian icons that gave the recurring patterns their name. Certainly in the Tibetan texts the first visions after the Light are mandalas of deities who come forth from them to present themselves. They will only be relevant to those brought up in those traditions, but high dose L.S.D. sessions have shown that other individuals create their own mandalas from personal experiences and that will be the form visions take in the Chikai Bardo. The early visions in the Tibetan sequence are benefic, then after '7 days' they will swing to the opposite: as wrathful deities. Again remain detached, just observe, and do not engage with either sort of vision even if the benefic ones appeal, they will quicken the descent to the wrathful ones by dialectic change. Both relate to your past experiences and cannot harm you if detached. If in doubt remember your favourite deity or teacher.

SIDPA BARDO

As, or if, karmic attachment involves you you will progress into the next level of experience called the Sidpa Bardo, when you feel as if you are possessed of supernatural power, like being able to travel great distances, or walk through walls. Don't engage with bardo beings who try to make you use these powers. You may well see visions of your old Earthly haunts and loved ones, but you cannot engage with them. Your journey is alone now. Visualise your favourite deity or teacher on the crown of your head to guide you.

Judgement Scenes:

You are bound to experience some form of judgement scenes, possibly with objectified bardo figures counting back and white marbles while reviewing your past life, or you just see visions where you judge your own past actions 'pro' or 'anti'. Try not to attach to negativity of judgement: it will colour your progress to future lives, but may be inevitable if strong events have left you with a guilty conscience. Desire for worldly wealth will lead you to the realm of hungry ghosts.

The Six Worlds: [the return of the Six Lights.]

Different colours will now appear as a result of the judgements:

Dull white lights leads to the realm of pleasure seeking gods
Dull yellow lights lead to the realm of rational humans
Dull green to the realm of warring giants
Dull blue to the realm of wild animals
Dull red to the realm of wandering unhappy spirits
Dull grey leads to the purging hell realms

As you follow these you are heading to rebirth.
Remember and visualise your favourite deity or teacher
Keep a positive outlook
Oppose bad karmic memories that seek to close the womb door around you
Ask for guidance from Mother-Father deities you can identify with
If in your visions of copulating couples you are drawn to the woman, you will be born male
If you are drawn to the man you will you will be born female
To prevent rebirth meditate on this as illusionary

The Continents of Rebirth

If your visions show a lake with swans, you will be born in the East
If of grazing horses, the West
If of trees and cattle, North
If impressive mansions, the South

Visions of Future Type of Existence

Temples: with the God/esses
Ring of Fire: Warring giants
Caves, burrows, pits, or seas: animals
Barren deserts, thick forests or jungles: Hungry Ghosts
Sirens singing enchanting songs: the purging hell realms
If you see a lotus enter it: avoiding bad karma and a giving a good birth. Meditate on your guardian deity or teacher
A favourable womb smells sweet, enter, meditate on yourself as Light. **OM MANE PADME HUM.**

Extreme Reactionaries:[No Satan in Tantrika]

Increasingly, on Facebook, I have been getting messages from people who imply that they are Satanists, but have been curious about what the Uttara stream of practice has to offer. So I need to make it clear that there is no connection between serious Tantrik practice and Satanism. The guru line teachings on this are quite clear. Tantrika is a stream of activity in Indian history which stands in opposition to the dominant Vedic practices, and probably has morphed out of the remnants of pre-Aryan invasion folk practice, as the Agamas, although the first treatises labelled Tantras were Vishnu, so Aryan, Tantras. After so long there are crossovers but pure Tantrika stands in opposition to Vedic impositions. That much it does have in common with Satanism, in that it is a reaction to imposed doctrines. Satanism, as such is merely the inversion of Christianity and means nothing without it. It is a later reaction against a borrowed monotheism which emerged after about 300 C.E., once it was the Emperor's new clothes for Roman Imperialism which chose to demonise the old gods by creating a bad guy to fulfil the dualism which makes a nonsense of monotheism. Generally referred to as 'the Devil', but with other associated 'bad guy' ideas dragged out of Middle Eastern mythology, like Lucifer. A satan was the Jewish name for 'a plotter', and on a theological scale he was the plotter against the monotheistic god. More recently we have seen Egyptian Set, the opposer, and Shaitan, desert demon of sand storms, tossed in to the pot boiler. The demonising imagery for concocting this devil was usually borrowed from old pagan figures like Pan or Kernunnos, with their horns of plenty. None of this affected Tantrika because monotheism never took a big hold in India or in surrounding countries until quite late and then in a way that managed to harmonise with existing conditions. Dominant Vedic culture was still pagan and paganism provides a choice as to how you view your deity, not the fanaticism of monotheism, which then went into endless arguments about whose version of that god was the correct one.

The most recent additions into the naming of monotheism's bad guy, as Set or Shaitan come from imaginative pen of Kenneth Grant. Set, the opposer of his Egyptian brother of legend creates an all male dualism which is a perfect conflict model, while Shaitan a storm god was obviously the enemy of desert people who suffered 'his' disruptive stormy arrivals. So both provide an archetype for opposition to order and will appeal to anarchic types who thrive on chaos and live in the shadow of that which they seek to oppose. Nothing to oppose, nothing to cast a shadow. Grant's derivations are chosen to suit his own personal psychology, [Pluto, lord of the Underworld rising and a mess of planets in his 8th house] and are often to lacking in historic reality, such as when he tried to connect 'An', an old name for Siva, to Set to create Set-an, a connection that never occurred anywhere except in Grant's mind. However his authoritative style of writing, backed by a chequered association with Aleister Crowley and his followers, lent Satan a new respectability for those who fancied themselves as sophisticated occultists opposed to usually a Christian priesthood as was Grant's father. Set-an is pure linguistic invention. But due to his authoritative tone of writing many people have been led into thinking that there was a connection between his Typhonian speculations and Tantrika.

Dadaji was quite clear that if you had no need for Jesus in your life then Satan also doesn't exist either. He becomes an irrelevance without the figure whose shadow he exists in. Both are presented as male and again gives the perfect model for conflict. The polarity in Tantrika, especially the Kaula, shakti cults, is male and female, representing the two primordial forces of nature in synergy: yin and yang that resolve into the Tao with correct practice as shakti energy is brought to bear to bring about union with the Absolute. An all male universe can't exist: it is infertile, and male dominant Patriarchal misery cults have become the curse of the planet. "Siva without Shakti is a shava" [corpse] is the old Hindu epithet. We can do little better in positive reaction against Patriarchy than to honour the Mother of the Universe in all her aspects. The only demons you will encounter in the Uttara tradition are your own, as you exorcise them on the path to liberation.

It is easy to see why people want to react against Christianity and Patriarchal cults, after Crusades, Inquisitions, and other 'holy' wars, but we don't need the extremes when it is possible to revert to Pagan expressions of the horned gods like Pan or Kernunnos, who is identical with Siva Pashupatinath of the Indus Valley civilisation, and the pagan Goddesses. These nature based ways of life do relate to Tantrika and by-pass the patriarchal eras.

For every revolution there will always be a counter revolution. For every action, a reaction. That is the dialectical principle known at least since Socrates' teacher identified it. I am quite happy to be part of that counter revolution and point to the absurdities that have grown out of 21st century Shaitanism, just as Dadaji did.

"There seems an unaccountable prepossession among all persons, to imagine that whatever seems gloomy must be profound, and whatever is cheerful must be shallow. They have put poor philosophy into deep mourning, and given her a coffin for a writing desk, and a skull for an ink stand."

Edward Bulwer-Lytton.

Yggdrasil
ODIN'S TREE OF VISION

East-West and Wica.

The real roots of what is called witchcraft are to be found in what has broadly been categorised as Shamanism, although the term was originally applied to Siberian individuals who acted as intermediaries with energies of expanded consciousness that informed the ancient tribes of Europe and Asia, for healing and transcendental knowledge. Similar functionaries can of course be found on other continents too, and are often referred to popularly as 'medicine men and women'. At the end of the 19th century, as historic prohibitions placed on such people began to wane, various claimants to hidden and usually hereditary knowledge began to step out of the shadows of anonymity, and to become the subject of academic interest to anthropologists like Dr. Margaret Murray [1863-1963] leading to what became known as Modern Witchcaft. Margaret was herself born in Kolkata in India, so was aware of Horned Gods, East and West: from the ancient one of Mohenjo-Daro in the Indus Valley that has been called Siva Pashupatinath: Lord of the Animals, as they surround him on an ancient Indus stele, to Kernunnos in the caves of Southern France. She was also the first female lecturer in England to teach archaeology, and worked at the prestigious University College of London.

We have noted elsewhere that Dadaji Mahendranath said he had his first initiation into witchcraft, aged 12, from his Great Aunt 'Clay', a hereditary witch who lived in a village near Brighton, England, and mentioned that his involvement with Gerald Brosseau Gardner, aka Scire [1884-1964] at the time of the latter's 'witchcraft centre' and nudist colony in Hertfordshire that has been confirmed by records. Gardner is usually referred to as the Father of Modern Witchcraft. We need to be careful as to what is implied by this term and what it actually means. Although he claimed to have been initiated by a coven of hereditary witches in the New Forest in Brighton's neighbouring county, scholars like Ronald

Hutton have shown that these people Gardner met through a Rosicrucian group had only been involved in witchcraft since the 1930s. As an amateur anthropologist and archaeologist Gardner had many esoteric interests, and many of the words used in his 'Book of Shadows' [1949] show these influences, not least of all from Freemasonry: such as 'a cable tow', in his cult used to bind witches to the altar in initiations, and the names Joachim and Boaz who give their name to pillars in masonic temples. Aleister Crowley's quabalistic re-spelling of the word of power 'abrahadabra' also appears amongst poems and songs of feasting and celebration. Influences from other ritual magic, rather than folk magic, creep in and ideas based on the modern anthropological ideas of witch history provided by Margaret Murray can be found. So it would appear that rather than rediscovering witchcraft he, to a large extent, invented modern wica [his spelling].... but certainly did a lot to publicise what evolved into the types of contemporary craft.

Gerald, a Lancashire boy originally, grew up partly in Madeira, and then Ceylon, now called Sri Lanka, then worked in Malaya in a colonial rubber plantation capacity. His career as a promoter of witchcraft really began after he retired in 1936. While in Cyprus he wrote a novel, 'The Goddess Arrives'. It was in 1939, while belonging to the Rosicrucian Order, the Crotona Fellowship, that he met the people in the group who initiated him into a witchcraft coven of sorts, when they took him to the house of Dorothy Clutterbuck of Highcliffe in the New Forest. Ronald Hutton's research has shown that they formed as a group in the 1930s using Margaret Murray's anthropological research, written up in such tomes as 'The God of the Witches' to inform their practices, rather than with anyone's hereditary knowledge. Since the persecutions of the Puritan era in Oliver Cromwell's 'Commonwealth' that suspended the British monarchy after beheading Charles I, witches had gone underground to avoid detection and hanging, so usually functioned as solitary herbalist Wise Women, often midwives, and Cunning Men, who all functioned as herbalist folk doctors. If covens did meet they met secretively in remote locations and were made up of those who could trust each other to not betray any of the group. Witchcraft among the wealthy elite as a parlour game was not unknown however. The laws against the Craft were not finally lifted until 1951, and that timing is very relevant to the resurgence that Gardner did much to create. After then a few real hereditary witches started to show their faces and gave a variety of descriptions of what practices had been used, often not as prescriptive as Gardner's, described in his 'Book of Shadows'.

While living in London after the war in 1945 Gardner started writing about his craft: in 1949, it was 'High Magic's Aid' first, which leaned heavily on ceremonial quabalistic magic, while 'the Book of Shadows' written in that year was his rule book for his covens; in 1954 it was 'Witchcraft Today' and in 1959 'The Meaning of Witchcraft'. Other members of his coven, such as Doreen Valiente also wrote on the subject. Gardner also met and influenced Ross Nichols who went on to found the Order of Bards, Ovates and Druids, mainly from Roman records, which were not sympathetic, and Gardner attended Stonehenge solstice rituals with the Ancient Druid Order, which was anything but ancient.

After the war had ended Gardner had also bought a nudist centre of four acres at Bricket Wood , near Watford in Hertfordshire, north of London, and had a 16th century cottage moved and re-erected there as a centre for his coven activities. It was opened with readings from the Key of Solomon, a grimoire of ritual magic with Middle Eastern connections rather than native folk magic. He joined an Esoteric Christian group in 1946, an anathema to pagans: then more appropriately the Folk Lore Society, and the Society for Psychical Research. He met Aleister Crowley in 1947 and was admitted to the 4th Degree of his OTO. He even became head of that order when Crowley died, before Karl Germer took over. He was nothing if not eclectic! It was at this time at Bricket Wood, in 1959, that Anton Miles, aka Dadaji, arrived to check out Gardner's set up, looking for like-minded people that he could share his hereditary knowledge with. How much that was so is not on record, but he only stopped ten weeks. Nudity was welcomed to strengthen bodily magical energies and followed him to India in his Nath days with its more welcoming climate for such pursuits, but some of the practices prescribed by Gardner like flagellation and being bound to the altar at initiations, owes more to bondage, albeit to deities, and domination, by priest/esses, than free Will and Liberation which Anton later promoted in India. Its easy to guess at Gardner's schooldays and the kind of authority figures he grew up with. Blindfolding at initiation is certainly borrowed from Freemasonry. Yet they continued to write to each other when Anton was in Australia, and Dadaji's westernised oaths for Nath and Uttarakaula initiations do owe a lot to Gardner's style of writing.

In 1947 and 48 Gardner toured in the U.S. and made able converts like Raymond Buckland, who went on to write '*The Tree, the Complete Book of Saxon Witchcraft*' which was well researched and singly focussed on its content's sources, with no bondage involved! It was published in 1974 by Weiser, after the 1960's 'Permissive Society' explosion when the Vietnam War and the over-arching threat of nuclear annihilation had led many to lose faith in Christianity in a way that caused people to look for less hypocritical paths. Buckland also called his book a Book of Shadows, after the reputed spell and ritual record books of witches of the Middle Ages used to record hidden details in a time of the other persecutions against witchcraft. But he said there were then no secrets and that the contents were open for all to follow since the lifting of legal restrictions in 1951 in England. He wasn't the only 'authority' to reveal the Craft's inner workings. Immigrants in the U.S. at the time of colonisation brought the elder faith with them and gradually began to reveal their heritage. Gardner's publicity spread across the States in the '50s and '60s, as well as Australia, with Dadaji's and local witch and artist Roseleen Norton's help, amongst others. Back in London after his travels Gardner got to know Austin Spare and Kenneth Grant by frequenting Atlantis Bookshop.

Further north and west, betwixt the other Celtic countries of Ireland and Wales, the Isle of Man, with its own People's Parliament of ancient tradition, drew the attention of Gardner and other fellow witch promoter, Cecil Williamson, so they attempted to set up the Museum of Magic and Witchcraft, but it proved unpopular and Gardner moved it to Boscastle, in equally Celtic, Cornwall, where it runs as a tourist attraction in the summer months into the 2020s at least.

There soon became off-shoots from Gardner when it came to setting up covens. As well as past priestesses from his own coven the two best known of those set up by males were Alex Sanders' [1926-88] from Merseyside, who claimed, when living across the estuary in Bethesda, North Wales to have been initiated by his grandmother, a hereditary hedge [solo] witch. He seems to have had some clairvoyant power which he used in a Spiritualist church and when studying Ceremonial magic. After his association with Gardner's coven he followed roughly the same model, watered down silk whip floggings and all, but with a strong quabalistic ceremonial element built in. After a move to London's Notting Hill and a later split from his wife, Maxine, she carried on the group as Alexandian witches.

Roy Bowers, a London draughtsman, aka Robert Cochrane [1931-66] on the other hand, after his own association with Gardner became very reactionary, and replaced nudity with black hooded robes, and required no flogging at all for allegiance to his Clan of Tubal Cain, a biblical name which makes amusing scrutiny. Tubal Cain like his forebear of the same name some 300 years earlier, in this borrowed Mesopotamian genealogy, as brother of Abel, the other son of Adam and Eve, had the name Cain, a variant of Qayin, or smith, indicating workers in metals. So at the earliest then the Bronze Age emerging, making it around 300 years from 'Creation' and the Garden of Eden to the beginnings of metallurgy. Cochrane's claims to hereditary lineage also proved to be false. Having Doreen Valiente from Gardner's coven for a member of his group for a while also led to strife, and an affair with a coven member ruined his marriage. So eventually he took to a long and painful suicide with a mixture of belladonna and sleeping pills. Quite a magus! Shani Oates, also a one-time Gardnerian, keeps the clan going far more successfully.

From the 1960s all manner of varieties of witch-like groups began to grow in the British Isles: Norse, Anglo Saxon, Celtic, Druid, Earth Magic, most with reverence for nature and herbal knowledge, reflecting the variety of shamanistic origins. Few bothered to claim hereditary connections but based their activities on published sources and anthropological research. One man with the most far-reaching knowledge of natural cycles headed a Celtic group in Scotland calling himself Kaledon Naddair. He had taken "the poetic intuitions" of author Robert Graves [1895-1985], the son of an Irish Celtic Revivalist, in his book 'The White Goddess', about the Celtic Tree Alphabet, based on nature's cycles and, by placing the Coelbren letters in the correct solar cross [a curvy swastika] found the formula for annual cycles of all native fauna and flora: knowledge of which had been wiped out by the Romans along with the Druids. Oddly he did also work the quabala into his calculations too, and that is Middle Eastern in origin, but obviously archetypal.

Meanwhile in 1961 in Australia Anton Miles, aka Dadaji, was receiving the attention of the Pictorial newspaper of Sydney reporting his early wanderings in the East, as a Buddhist [no explicit name for what variety was given, but probably just a local Aussie group] and as a witch who knew Gardner, who he still wrote to, and Crowley, in England. He and his girlfriend said they worshipped Pan and Diana, rather than Kernunnos and Aradia of the Gardner coven. Rosaleen Norton, 'the Witch of Kings Cross' was also active and infamous in Sydney at the time, and Anton knew her too, but thought her, like all quabalistic pathworkers, as an 'astral junkie' despite her amazing paintings and drawings based on trance visions. He had also learned witchcraft in native style in Siam, at that time a mix of 21st century Thailand and Burma. I have visited a cave temple dedicated to both Siva and the Buddha near the River Kwai in Thailand: one that had been used to house Japan's prisoners of war for railway line building in World War II, that Dadaji told Kristen Godfrey he had visited, after restoration of wartime damage.

Back in Essex in the '80s when Dadaji's travels were all but over and groups were forming to put the lessons of the travels into some comprehensible form, our local group began to look into our own native heritage in tandem with the Eastern revelations. The town of Chelmsford is the centre of the County of Essex and so became the county town. That meant that in the Puritan era of Cromwell's Commonwealth, 1649 to 1660, it held the assizes where Witchfinder General, Matthew Hopkins', victims were brought to trial and then the gallows, by being dragged the 20 miles from the hell hole that was the dungeon of Colchester Castle. Earlier, in King Edward VI's short reign Dr. John Dee had been at boarding school in Chelmsford too before he became Edward's sister, Queen Elizabeth I's, astrologer and espionage agent. In fact the trumped-up witch laws created by Edward and Elizabeth's father, the infamous Henry VIII, to accuse his second wife Anne Boleyn of witchcraft as evidence towards her beheading, were still being used for trials of Hopkins victims. So the aura of those executions still hung over the town. As the centuries rolled on witches went underground and the county of Essex saw several Cunning Men and Wise Women of note who survived the law before the repealing of the witchcraft laws in 1951.

Foremost amongst these was Old George Pickingill [1816-1909], on the face of it a farm labourer from the village of Canewdon, just north of Southend, but legend had it there were always seven successive witches in the village, and George had a lineage traceable to the Norman Conquest of 1066, and a female forebear who tried to defeat the Normans by witchcraft. He was also head of nine covens through East Anglia: Essex, Suffolk, Norfolk and Cambridgeshire, plus ones in Hampshire and Sussex that we mentioned in relation to Gardner's witch beginnings, if not to people related to Pickingill. Old George was known to have advised Gardner as well as Aleister Crowley, who was initiated into one of George's Norfolk covens. George also advised Freemasons, Rosicrucians and even Cambridge academics. Sex magic certainly came into his circles, in Canewdon and other churchyards, not as desecration: but because churches were often built on old pagan sites like crossroads of ley lines. He was quite amoral in his outlook and would curse if he thought it needs be. However Pickingill's covens did confirm that not all witches had been solitary practitioners during the secrecy that followed persecutions, that went much further back than those of the Puritan era.

Another prominent Cunning man from Essex was James Murrell [1812-1860] who operated in the Hadleigh area near Southend, and could be encountered on his nocturnal rambles in search of herbs or helping Moonrakers [smugglers] of the Thames estuary. He was said to practice only benign magic, often counter magic against people who had laid curses, or exorcising troublsome spirits. He was the seventh son of a seventh son, often said to be the mark of a witch. His staff was his umbrella: a much needed tool for herb gathering in the climate of the misty Thames estuary. Other paraphenalia were known to include a scrying mirror, witches bottles, a copper dowsing rod, and a talismanic pendant. Other Essex Cunning Folk are recorded as having been found in Barking, Billericay, Colchester and Tendring. Old Mother Redcap was a common name for Wise Women, who often carried a red medicine bag. So by the time our group became active in the County there was a strong tradition to set the background scenery for our activities.

As we were an East-West group, at the behest of Dadaji, we too began a circle on the local common of Galleywood in the 1980s and '90s. There were actually two or three circles interactive in the area, but our main 'coven' was of four members, one for each element: to call the Quintescent Ones. A Lady of Shakti was attended by myself, a biker, and by turns first a wood carver and then a dreadlocked grown Punk who I had known at his school that I worked at briefly. We chose the site by intuition. I emphasised the 'ley' part of Galleywood because we knew it was a ley line [Old English for a 'meadow': a clearing in woods at junctures of lines of Earth's magnetic energy used by Druids and akin shamans]. But we walked around until the circle presented itself: with a mountain ash tree at it's centre, around which animals had created a circular track. Spot-on! I cast the circle with a sword stick, 'air', where the blade slid into the stick to be less obvious while travelling en-route [although one dog walker did once get the fright of his life!]; a wax torch brand, 'fire'; stone chalice, 'water'; and incense burner for 'earth'. No fancy robes: an East Anglian tradition is that if coats are turned inside out the sprites will not recognise mortals [see Nigel Pennick: *'Secrets of East Anglian Magic'* and *'Practical Magic in the Northern Tradition'*]. The circle was opened with three perambulations. I invoked Siva as the Pan/Kernunnos dialect with "Iao Pan!" He came clairaudinently with the sound of hoofbeats. We found out later that the nearest road to the site was called Goat Hall Lane! We were all involved in Green politics and the workings were always for ecological issues....and with Pan's help, very successfully. As many will know, group magic is far stronger than solo, and then add ten fold for being in nature at a focal point of earth energies. The circle was closed by three ambulations in reverse direction. We observed solstices and equinoxes at first and then extended to cross-quarter days too. Other rituals were left for couples and individuals in their domestic surroundings. It was unfortunate that with time members moved to different locations that made meetings impossible after a while.

A local pub was frequented by Punks, Bikers and Hippies, and one client was the late James McNess, a convener for Traditional Witchcraft gatherings, and Andrew Chumbley took initiation from him, then formed another group that was the beginnings of Cultus Sabbati. The group consisted of three couples: him and his partner; his partner's brother and wife, married in Nepal. She was an able artist and produced much splendid artwork for the Typhonian OTO'S magazine. A third couple, close friends of Chumbley and his wife, split because of his egocentric domineering manner, but then soon after that the husband was exposed for downloading pornographic images of children! The biker from our group worked with Chumbley and McNess at times. So did a fella who had pseudo Druid and Dion Fortune spin-off groups connections.

Generally the Cultus group used some variant of a traditional craft group like Gardner's with three degrees: a degree of joining, a degree of learning how to use magical tools, and the High Priestess and Priest grade. Prof. Ronald Hutton, correctly I'm sure, said that these three grades are taken from Freemasonry: the primary three craft grades, after which one passes under the Royal Arch to many higher degrees. Similarly there are three levels of practice that are those of the householders in the Kula family and clan. Beyond that there are six more levels of practice for wielding planetary powers that are usually reserved for when family responsibilities are discharged, but can be accessed previously if needs require it. The first three grades however vary in the kaulas to those in masonry and Gardnerism in that the experiments of sex life and its transcendental virtues in the kula family takes place in the second level of practice, while in Gardner's model the Priestess and Priest perform 'the Great Rite' in the third degree, symbolically or otherwise, at Sabbats. The third level of practice in Kula such activities continue, especially in relation to the Sri Yantra, but should be the time of mature fulfilment generally. That doesn't mean that it is top loaded, as illumination can come at any level. Yet both East or West can see each other's general parallels, even if one is about learning a craft and the other, where individual dharma is equated with expanding levels of consciousness.

The Universe: the 0=2 Equation

When Lawrence Miles, later to be best known as Dadaji Mahendranath, met Aleister Crowley in the last years of his life he was in some respects a jaded old junkie who didn't display the willpower that he portrayed himself with in *'Diary of a Drug Fiend'* to overcome his addiction to the cosy glow of the pain-relieving medicine he had come to rely on. Yet his intellect was certainly not diminished and the man that Dadaji found was a Taoist scholar working on translations of the *Tao Te Ching* and *I Ching*, and one who advised him to go East in his search for such esoteric knowledge, which he did eventually do, visiting Malaysia and Myanmar/Thailand: Siam, where Taoism still thrived alongside Buddhism, before backtracking to India.

In one of Crowley's letters that were assembled to create the book *'Magick Without Tears'* he demonstrates a fine grasp of the Taoist cosmology as against many other philosophies. That has great bearing on Shakti Tantra, as it shows equal respect for female participants to that accorded the males. It is Chinacara.

Crowley begins with philosophical axioms:

We are aware.

We cannot doubt the existence of something, real or illusory, because doubt itself is a form of awareness.

We group together all that we are aware of as 'existence': to call it a 'cosmos', implies 'order', and that may not be so.

We assume that there are things in existence we are not aware of, be that so or not. Something appears to be, and seems to be incalculably vast and complex, so we ask "How did this come to be?" This then is the 'Riddle of the Universe'.

Such replies, posing as an answer, are likely to be "God created it", leading to the question "Who created God?". Perhaps God is a demi-urge then, a front man for something of eternal, formless greatness...this gets us no further. Explanations like the universe being supported by an elephant, even that the elephant is himself standing on a tortoise, have been offered in this way to the naive.

Perhaps there are mother and father figures and elements involved then. Philosophers have then decided to categorise these schools of thought into nihilist, monist and pluralist. This last category seems promising as oriental schools studying the universe can easily identify 'pairs of opposites' such as Devas and Asuras, Osiris and Set, and other personifications of good and evil that can provide 'wars in heaven', grizzly places for one side, like hell, for one side and a shiny realm for saints and angels. A dying god to act as redeemer is then likely to bring salvation in with his omnipotence. The Monists, such as Advaitist Hindus are keen on an Ultimate reality of Brahman, a supreme being without qualities or quantities. All else is maya: illusion, yet 'religious experience' is used to support this theory where whatever personal god, Vishnu, Jesus or Mithras for instance, can appear to them in visions, but if all is illusion how can this be? Crowley's own philosophical system includes the 'knowledge and conversation of a personal guardian angel', called atmadharshana, it is a personal apprehensible universe as a single phenomenon without time, space or causality. That is his solution. To realize this is 'to make real' the notion of the monists, and normal life becomes an illusion while experiencing what the Hindus call Samadhi. Notions of an origin of the universe are of no consequence in such a condition. And even modern astro physics that created 'the big bang' theory just made the latest attempt to satisfy the old obsession with some kind of Creation. So 'two', or 'many' do not create origin, as they can be reduced to One and One can have no creator. This leads us to a form of positive nihilism, and Crowley then goes into the advanced mathematics of zero, but kindly provides an explanation using logic which is easier to comprehend than the algebraic abstractions. Both lead to the beautiful simplicity of the Chinese philosophy which begins with absolute zero: 0 to the power of 0, and they do give it a name: the Tao. But to assert nothing is not to explain the universe, so they say that nothing means nothing: it has no qualities or quantities. Advaitism does the same but calls it 1, but the Chinese say that it is always possible to reduce anything to nothing by adding 2 equal and opposite things: n+[-n]= 0. So they began to diagrammatize the Universe as the 1 with a pair of opposites: the Yang active, 'male' and the Yin passive, 'female', the Yang an unbroken line [-] and Yin a broken line [- -]. The names given to these are Thai Yang, the Sun, and Thai Yin, the Moon. By doubling these glyphs they arrived at the four Hsiang : 2 unbroken lines; 2 broken lines; 1 broken above and 1 unbroken line below; one unbroken above with a broken line. Then three at a time they arrived at the eight Pa Kwa trigrams:

Male		1	[Ch'ien]		[Heaven,Father]

Male   1   [Ch'ien]   [Heaven,Father]
Female   1   [Kun]   [Earth, Mother]
Male2   [Li]   [Sun]
Female 2   Kan [Moon

Male 3   Kan [Fire]

                                   Female 3   Tui [Water]

Male 4   Sun [Air]

                                   Female 4   Ken [Earth]

TRIGRAMS UPPER ▶ / LOWER ▼	Ch'ien	Chên	K'an	Kên	K'un	Sun	Li	Tui
Ch'ien	1	34	5	26	11	9	14	43
Chên	25	51	3	27	24	42	21	17
K'an	6	40	29	4	7	59	64	47
Kên	33	62	39	52	15	53	56	31
K'un	12	16	8	23	2	20	35	45
Sun	44	32	48	18	46	57	50	28
Li	13	55	63	22	36	37	30	49
Tui	10	54	60	41	19	61	38	58

So the original has developed into the four elements, which balance perfectly against each other.

By doubling the Pa Kwa they achieve the 64 hexagrams of the I Ching: a map of the elements and their interaction. The numbers in the chart above are the chapters of the I Ching.

All this unfolding and 0 being equal to [plus -] + [minus -]

... Just as life unfolds from an act of love that creates a child, real or magickal, and parents relax into ecstasy of zero in a concept-less void......until the nappies need changing!

Louis Culling an American follower of Crowley founded a

magickal order [The Great Brotherhood of God!] basing all its workings on the 64 hexagams which, when consulted as an oracle, determined how male and female would conjoin. Hardly the sophisticated methods of the Taoist Love manuals, but two good examples of how they apply are Hexagram 11, 'Peace' which shows the Kali Asana with the Goddess on top, for maximum clitoral stimulation, and Hexagram 12, 'Stagnation' where the male is on top, as in the missionary position!

A good starting point for looking at traditional Chinese Taoist lovemaking texts is
'The Tao of Love and Sex' by Jolan Chang ISBN 9780140193381.
0 = [+1]+[-1] IS THE KEY TO ALL TAOIST SEX MAGIC: 0 IS AN ELECTRIC CIRCUIT
+1 AND -1 ARE THE POSITIVE AND NEGATIVE POLES OF CURRENT THAT CREATE IT.

At an atomic level Shakti is electrons, while Siva is the nucleus.

Anulama Krama and Biloma Krama

Anulama Krama is the ascending order of the male basal energy
symbolised by a phallic snake: the so-called right-hand path.
Biloma Krama is the descending order, where female shakti
energy descends from the Sahasrara crown to to the mulhadhara
centres before returning to the Sahasrara: the left-hand path.

APPENDICES:

Charters.

Dadaji's 1979 designations for a Westernised Uttarakaula Order.

Some background reading.

ORIENTAL TANTRIK ORDER.

PROMULGATUS POPULUS:

BE IT KNOWN, UNDERSTOOD AND ACCEPTED, THAT ON THIS DAY, THE FIFTH OF APRIL, 1979, BECAUSE WE ARE ON THE THRESHOLD OF A NEW AEON, AND BECAUSE OF THE DIRE NEED FOR A WESTERN AND ORIENTAL ORGANISATION OF TANTRIKS IN THE ENTIRE WORLD, THIS DECISION — BEING MY TRUE WISH AND WILL, SHALL FROM THIS DATE BECOME EFFECTIVE.;

THEREFORE, I , SHREE GURUDEV 'DADAJI" MAHENDRANATH 999, SOLE GURU AND SURVIVING PRECEPTOR OF THE UTTRAKAULA TANTRIKS OF INDIA, DO HEREBY INSTITUTE AND GIVE FORM TO A NEW INTERNATIONAL, ESOTERIC AND ARCANE MAGICK ORDER TO BE KNOWN AS THE

ORIENTAL TANTRIK ORDER or (O.T.O.)

THIS ORDER, HAVING ITS ROOTS IN ANCIENT INDIA AND THEREBY FROM CENTURY OLD CUSTOM, BE DIVIDED INTO NINE GRADES AND THAT THE FIRST INITIAL INITIATION OF A NEW MEMBER BE GIVEN BY NAKED GURU TO NAKED SISHYA OF EITHER SEX. THE ORIENTAL TANTRIK ORDER SHALL OPERATE AS AN AUTONOMOUS SUPRA-PARTICLE AND AN ACTIVE SEGMENT OF THE CONCORD OF COSMIC PEOPLE. IT WILL THUS GIVE DIVINE ADHESION FOR STAR PEOPLE WHOM WISH TO DEVELOP THEIR LATENT POWERS IN COSMIC ART, WITH ITS DECORATIVE AND INSPIRING SOUND AND VISION, IN INSTRUMENTS OR VOICE, OR TO TAKE SHAPE IN METAL OR STONE OR ON PAPER, PARCHMENT, PUBLIC WALLS, PAVEMENTS AS WELL AS ON THE SKIN OF THE HUMAN BODY. THE ORIENTAL TANTRIK ORDER DEFINES ITS ESOTERIC INITIATION RITES, WORK AND OBJECTIVES AS — THE PATH OF EXPRESSION AND LIBERATION OF THE MIND THROUGH CREATIVE ENJOYMENT — THE GRAND MASTER OF THE ORDER SHALL LEAD SELECTED AND AWAKENED COSMIC PEOPLE THE THE HIGHEST POWERS OF MAGICK THROUGH DIVINE AND EROTIC ECSTACY AND THE TANTRIK WAY OF LIFE.
THUS DO WE DIFINE THE ORDER AND ITS PURPOSE.

THEREFORE, TO FINALISE THIS DECISION AND THE SUBSTANCE OF THE ORDER, I DO HEREBY DESIGNATE, APPOINT AND ORDAIN AS THE FIRST GRAND MASTER, WHOSE INSTRUCTIONS AND CONSTRUCTION WILL BE FINAL:

SIR JOHN POWER, SUPREME ARTISTA OF THE PHANTASIA AND THE PHANTASMAGORIA OF THE COSMIC PEOPLE; WHOM I NAME AND SPRINKLE WITH AMBROSIA AS SHRI VILĀSANATH; MAGE OF SARASWATI AND MINERVA; PRIEST-LORD OF KĀMARŪPA; SAGE-KING OF KAILĀSA; ARCHITECT OF BIFROST, THE RAINBOW BRIDGE LINKING OUR PAGAN KINGDOM WITH THE COSMOS AND ASTRO-INTELLIGENCES AND THE SPACE-SCRIBES OF MANDALAS, CHAKRAS, SYMBOLS, DIAGRAMS AND EROTICA.

THAT WHICH IS DONE IS DONE FOR THE WEAL AND WELFARE OF ALL MANKIND AND THE ENJOYMENT OF THE PEOPLE OF REAL PEACE, REAL FREEDOM AND REAL HAPPINESS. THIS IS OUR NATURAL LAW AND THE RHYTHM OF THE COSMOS BY WHICH THE WISE MUST LIVE.

THE WILL TO LOVE IS THE LAW TO LIVE!

SIGNED 5/4/79.   Mahendranath.

Fellowship of Uttara Circles of Kaulas
1.3.20
Update of previous charters

Om Ganesh!
guide and protect us in our rites
and as you will.

Hrim Lalita!

Further to previous charters, now let there be greater clarity:
where previous charters spoke of uniting the twin streams of
Adi Nath and Uttarakaula householders in the West
as seemed the later wishes of Sri Gurudev Dadaji Mahendraneth,
who until his death, was head of both streams, and thought he was last remaining guru of both sects.
However it has since been found that Kulavadhut of Sikkim is lineage holder of the native
Uttarakaulas. So the Fellowship continues as Dadaji's adaptation of the tradition for Westerners.
We therefore offer concord to international lines of Adi Naths who have
remained true to Dadaji's adaptions of Hindu traditions,
and to the sister line from Maheshwari Ma/ Kulavadhut that needs no adaptation.
To groups that have evolved beyond Dadaji's initiatives
into independent forms we offer respect for their right to innovate,
while the Fellowship retains its independence from Native Indian Uttarakaulas and Naths
due to the line of Indian descent of Kulavadhut, making a Nath/Uttara merge unnecessary.
***
Therefore I confirm Gregory Peters, Uttaranasetu Indrayudam Nath, aka Ajeyanath,
to lead the continuation of
East-West fusion of the Uttarakaula line,
after I leave mortal life.
Cliff Berns, Nimesanath, and Leila Rose, Tripura Sundari Devi
are also empowered to help by performing initiations if needs be.
Any previous charters except Dadaji's of 1979, on this matter now become void.

***

So be it in the lineage of
Pagal Haranath, Thakar Kalachand, Pagalababa of Ranchi, and Dadaji Mahendranath,

while Kula Avadhut continues the line from Thakar Kalachand, and Maheshwari Ma in India.

***
The rites, work and objectives of the Fellowship in the West remain the Path of Expression and
Liberation of the Mind through Creative Enjoyment in a fusion of Eastern and Western traditions.

So mote it be in Thelema.
Vilasanath
1.3.20

Om Namah Shivaya; Hreem Lalita Swaha!
Hrim Lalita,Swaha!

130

Dada ji's original designations for an Order of North Indian Tantriks of Aryadesha (India) with mystic values, 1979.

Degree	Planet	Earth Symbols	Grade of	Qualities	Level of	Devi	Degree of	Colour Symbol	Worship by
1°=9°	Sun	Circle	Day	Wonder	Neophyte	Santoshi-ma	Elementary Shrine Worship	White Sunrise	Initiation & Instruction
2°=8°	Moon	Crescent	Night	Illumination	Polarity / Enchantment	Shanti	Kulachakra Circle	Yellow / Full Moon	Polarity & Union
3°=7°	Jupiter	Triangle	Guru	Wisdom	Divine Triangulation	Tripura	Philosophy / Triangles	Pink Sunset	Sex Symbols
4°=6°	Saturn	Square	Skulls Dispassion	Divine Depriation	Aghori	Revelation	Green Rainbow	Yantras & Mandalas
5°=5°	Mercury	Cup	Communication	Enjoyment – Naked	Nebulous Digambari	Gymnosophists of the Order	Blue Trees	The 5 Elements (senses)
6°=4°	Venus	Fire	Love Union	Auto-eroticism	Kali	The Primal Sacrifice	Scarlet Planets	Sexual Ritual
7°=3°	Venus	Stone	Mystery Oracle	Oracle & Ornament	Ambika	Dolls & Dancers	Crimson Zodiac	Mantras & meditation
8°=2°	Mars	Sword	Warrior	Conflict & Protection	Luminous Lustrations	Durga	Blood	Maroon Galaxy	Starfire
9°=1°	Neptune	Wand	Magician	Miraculous	Opus Magnum	Lalita	Magna Mater	Purple	Space (Akasha) Starfire	Silent Contemplation

131

SOME BACKGROUND READING:

Sakti and Shakta Sir John Woodroffe. Ganesh and Co. Madurai

Kularnava Tantra trans. Sansthan. Pradeep Kumar Ray, Varanasi.

Tantrasara of Abvinavagupta tran. Chakravarty, Rudra Press U.S.

Krama Tantricism of Kashmir Navjian Rastogi, Motilal Delhi

Ananda Lahari Commentary Sivananda, Bhattacharyaia Kolkata

Shakti the Power of Tantra Rajmani Tigunait, Himalayan Institute

The Light on Kailash Chogyal Namkai Norbu, Shang Shung, Italy

Beyond the Mauve Zone Kenneth Grant, Starfire, U.K.

The Magical Union of East and West Greg Peters, Llewellyn, U.S.

Nu Tantras of the Uttarakaulas John Power, Phoenix, U.K.

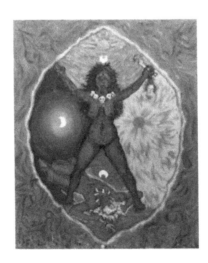

Lightning Source UK Ltd.
Milton Keynes UK
UKHW050413290122
397823UK00003B/15